CONCILIUM
Religion in the Seventies

CONCILIUM

New Series: Volume 1, Number 10: Sociology of Religion

THE CHURCH AS INSTITUTION

Edited by

Gregory Baum and Andrew Greeley

Herder and Herder

1974
HERDER AND HERDER NEW YORK
815 Second Avenue
New York 10017

ISBN: 0-8164-2575-2

Library of Congress Catalog Card Number: 73-6430

Printed in the United States

CONTENTS

PART III

THE SOCIOLOGY OF ECCLESIASTICAL INSTITUTIONS

Editorial

OVER the last decade the dialogue of theology with the social sciences has come to be regarded as highly significant. While theologians in the past tended to restrict their dialogue to the biblical sciences, history and philosophy, they have now become convinced that the study of Christianity, even from the viewpoint of the believer, demands an extensive conversation with the social sciences, especially sociology. It was for this reason that *Concilium* decided to devote one issue each year to such interdisciplinary studies.

We decided to designate the subject of these issues as "sociology of religion". It is of course very difficult to categorize studies that bring together various disciplines examining the phenomenon of religion—theology, sociology, psychology, etc.—for they fit into none of the recognized subdivisions of theology nor can they be identified with social science or any of its branches. To refer to the issues of *Concilium* devoted to this multidisciplinary approach as "sociology of religion" would be misleading were it not for the simple fact that these issues belong to a theological journal. They address themselves in the first place to theologians and students of theology. They appeal to Christians engaged in scholarly reflection on their religion. They intend to affect the theological self-understanding of the Christian community by introducing Christians to the critical method with which social science studies their religion and their religious institutions.

The "sociology of religion" issues are not primarily addressed to the professional sociologist and the researcher in the sociology of religion. They may none the less be of interest to the sociologist, for dialogue with theology has, in many instances, enabled the sociologist to approach the study of religion with more empathy and greater critical awareness, to clarify the overall perspective from which he examines his topic, and to ask new questions previously unknown to him, questions that have arisen in the self-understanding of the believing community. While the "sociology of religion" issues aim at helping the theologian and the student of theology to do their proper work, we hope that they will also be of interest to the sociologist.

The present issue, dealing with the Church as institution, does not require a detailed introduction. Since theologians are not in agreement about the social reality of the Church and since sociologists are not agreed on how to define "institution" and on the methods to be used in studying the social reality of religion, the first two introductory sections, respectively entitled "Theological Reflections" and "Sociological Orientations", introduce the reader to some of these diverse approaches. We are living at a time when sociologists are becoming more aware of the symbolic presuppositions operative in their scientific study of the social reality. The third and main section, entitled "The Sociology of Ecclesiastical Institutions", contains the greater part of the articles, each dealing with a particular aspect of the Church's institutional life, studied from the viewpoint of sociology. Many of these articles have important ecclesiological implications, but since they are written by sociologists, it will usually be up to the reader himself to extract the meaning of the sociological analysis for the better theological understanding of the Christian Church.

Andrew Greeley and I worked together on the preparation of this issue. We decided that for purposes of administrative efficiency we would alternate in assuming senior responsibility for the execution of the issue. I am therefore signing the editorial of this issue and Andrew Greeley will have senior responsibility in our joint enterprise next year.

GREGORY BAUM

PART I
THEOLOGICAL
REFLECTIONS

Gotthold Hasenhüttl

Church and Institution[1]

MOST of us were born into a Church with an institutional structure. All religious communities which call themselves churches
are in one form or another institutions. Today there are so many
suggestions for improving the institutional side of the Church
that this discussion now has an almost wearying effect. Nor does
this mean that the pressure the institution exercises on believing
men and women has become less—the weariness of the dialogue
is more like a sign of hopelessness. Suggestions for changing the
structures get bogged down and democratizing tendencies have
no result. The churches have not brought about many changes
and have, if anything, emptied them of content. The institution's
hold on power prevents a living growth of new practices and
ideas.

This situation forces us to ask what the relation of Church
and institution is. Is the Church an institution in its essence?

I. THE CHURCH'S UNDERSTANDING OF ITSELF

Without taking a particular definition of "institution" for
granted, we may note four essential institutional elements in the
Church. Where an authority occupies a pre-existing office and
enjoys a permanent title, we have an institution. Authority and
office are not challenged in the Church. What is discussed is

[1] For a detailed discussion see my *Kirche als Institution* (Freiburg,
1973).

purely and simply the way in which offices are exercised and the range of people from among whom they are filled. In the Catholic Church those holding office are also the administrators of the sacraments, the validity of which often depends on ordination. This gives the sacraments an unbreakable connection with the institution. Baptism, for example, was a practice, but became an official act, thus bringing about the institution of baptism. The eucharist acquired the label "divine" in itself, apart from its celebration, and thus became institutionalized. The sphere of law, which is controlled by the institution, is another essential institutional element in the Catholic Church. But the Church is not an institution merely in its functions as authority, hierarchy, administrator of the sacraments and legal body. It also possesses infallibility as an institution. Since this infallibility, which, according to a particular interpretation of the Bible, is peculiar to the Church, has a certain (charismatic) vagueness, it must, for the sake of efficiency, be tied down to the institution. This is the role of the dogma of infallibility. Through this not only the religious life, but also its ethical implications, are again completely subordinated to the institution. The key position has the authority ("the power of the keys"!). It is the highest authority and has its subjects. It is called hierarchy, "holy rule" or "domination" and has three main areas of power: (1) the sacraments; (2) legal competence; (3) the religious and moral lives of the faithful.

It is not necessary to describe here how the individual elements developed and gradually acquired more solid institutional form. The process reached a climax at the First Vatican Council. The dominant picture of the Church, in accordance with the newly defined dogma of infallibility, is well expressed in the draft Constitution on the Church, which was not in the end put to the vote: "The Church possesses all the characteristics of a true society. It is quite false to claim that Christ left this society undefined and without a fixed form. On the contrary, he himself gave it existence, his will determined the form of its existence and he gave it its *constitution*. . . . In itself it is so perfect as to be distinct from, and far superior to, all human associations" (Neuner-Roos, 361). There can be no doubt that the Roman Catholic hierarchy is meant by this term "constitution". In other words, Christ did not merely found the Church as an institution, but also instituted quite specific institutional elements.

The Second Vatican Council tried to reduce these claims, but nevertheless maintained quite clearly that the Church is an institution. Though there is true equality among all the faithful (Constitution, *Lumen Gentium*, on the Church, 32), a hierarchy nevertheless exists, in which the successor of Peter has supreme, complete, direct and universal power "over all the churches" (Decree, *Christus Dominus*, on the Bishops, 2). Even after the Second Vatican Council the nature of the Church as an institution remains unchallenged, and the power structures remain untouched, because the institution is identified mainly with the hierarchy, holy rule or domination in the Church. In the official Catholic view of the Church, the Church is not just an institution with particular elements (such as sacraments) which derive from an authoritative act of institution by Christ. It is also an institution to which power structures are necessary to salvation. An essential feature of the Church as institution is therefore superiority and subordination, different classes. The protests of so many theologians have so far done nothing to change this.

Among Protestants this sort of definition of the relations between Church and institution appears in a weaker form. There are tendencies which limit themselves to particular elements (preaching, two sacraments), or even only allow the institution conditional existence. The institution belongs (dialectically) to the Church as a response to certain needs. As a whole, however, Protestants do not deny that the Church is an institution. The remarkable opposition of Rudolf Sohm (1841–1917) received no support. Let us briefly examine Sohm's ideas.

II. THE NON-INSTITUTIONAL CHURCH

For Sohm, the Church was not an institution in its essence, indeed it betrays its essence as soon as it becomes one. His view was the precise opposite. Whereas for "Rome" the Church is an institution in its essence, for Sohm the Church of Christ was in no sense an institution. Every Christian receives his own gifts and his own charisma and these constitute the Church and create community. The spontaneity of Christians itself creates order.

Anyone who lives by the Spirit of God pays attention to others, and accepts them. If everyone does this, an ordered life comes into existence which is immune to the deadly paralysis of the institution. Nothing is laid down and everything develops through the actions of men. No one has a right to be obeyed in virtue of any official position, but acknowledgment of one's fellow Christians itself induces a degree of spontaneous mutual subordination. This guarantees a living system, but does not establish any institution out of which the domination of one man over another could emerge.

Since there is no formal authority, relations between the members are free from domination. Co-ordination is achieved, not by law, but by the Spirit of God through *charisma* or love in action.[2] The absence of an institution is the expression of a living community in which freedom and true equality prevail. As a result, there is no holy domination (hierarchy), but at the most a holy freedom from domination (a holy an-archy). A community filled with the Christian spirit lives by "pneumatic anarchism".[3] All organized political societies exercise power over their members, but the Church is constituted in its essence by its refusal to exercise power. For the Church of Christ at least, the governing principle is holy anarchy. Any adaptation to existing social conditions means that the Church is being untrue to its nature. The Spirit is suppressed or even extinguished. For this reason, it is wrong for the Church ever to become an institution.

III. WHAT IS AN INSTITUTION?

Both views on the relation between Church and institution see in the concept of institution a strong connection with domination. The meaning of the term itself is disputed. It is sometimes practically synonymous with human habits and sometimes it is used to denote an instrument for suppressing human freedom. The term derives its meaning from the attitude of the individual writer to institutions and can be used in a positive or a negative sense. Since the Church can be defined either in terms of an institution or in contrast to "institution", sociology of religion

[2] R. Sohm, *Kirchenrecht*, I (Leipzig, 1892), p. 495.
[3] *Idem, Wesen und Ursprung des Katholizismus* (Leipzig, [2]1912), p. 54.

needs a definition that will make an understanding of the Church possible. What, then, does "institution" mean? An *institution* is a *changeable*, but *permanent, product of purposive social role behaviour* which *subjects the individual to obligations*, gives him *formal authority* and possesses *legal sanctions*.

The word "institution" means, literally, something set up, established, formed and stable. Institutions are long-term creations. They are connected with man's existence in time, which means that they need time and are thus always human. Whatever attitude an institution may adopt towards people, it remains a human product. Theologians may want to protest here in case the Church, as an institution, may be suspected of being merely a human product. But Jesus founded neither the Church nor its institution—no act of founding can be found either in the Bible or in history—but merely made a new community possible by his call for faith and followers. This means that the institutional side of the Church, at least, is a human product. Even the Second Vatican Council lists as "human elements": "a society furnished with hierarchical agencies...a visible assembly", "the earthly Church" (Constitution on the Church, 8). The holy rule or domination, whose legitimacy cannot be questioned, is therefore a human product. This gives us grounds for calling all the institutional elements in the Church human products.

Anything produced by man can in principle be changed, and there is therefore no institution which is unchangeable, however slow and difficult these changes may be. Human freedom can transform it. The concept of institution includes the possibility of abolishing the institution.

This human product which is changeable but designed to last is not a private individual creation, but an intersubjective structure. The individual may have various habits, but we cannot talk of an institution until a relationship with a community has been created and an interhuman connection made. This social basis of action is expressed in the sacramental teaching of the Catholic Church. Institutional, sacramental acts can only be performed interpersonally, that is, in common. No one can baptize himself, absolve himself from guilt, ordain himself a priest or solemnize his own marriage.

The elements of the institution mentioned so far would probably be for the most part generally recognized and included in the definition of institution. The definition does not run into difficulties until patterns of behaviour are regarded as obligatory. In my view, we cannot speak of an institution in the full sense until we have reached this point.[4] Obligations give the human product a structure of demands. Obligations do not arise out of my spontaneous understanding or my wishes, but out of the action of someone else. This makes an institution essentially external control. It faces the individual as an external object and a source of pressure. The obligation which the institution imposes on the individual is the role. The role is the point at which the institution is lived. Institutions function through the action of individuals in playing their roles and identifying with them. Any refusal to accept the allotted role (in the Church to act as a layman or a cleric) is an attack on the institution. Anyone who transfers the obligations of the layman's role to a cleric or vice versa challenges the existing class distinctions within the Church and threatens the institution. The playing by individuals of their respective roles displays a differentiation of tasks and a variety of levels of authority.

This authority is given to the individual or the group, not as a result of special competence but in virtue of his prescribed role. The leading roles are played by those who are regarded as a guarantee of the relative permanence of the whole behaviour pattern. The obligations and corresponding rights of roles are confirmed by the authority of the leading roles, which rely for their force on a formalized set of gradations which is accepted as real. Role authority is necessary to every institution. This authority is not based on special competence, but is formal. The occupant of a position in the institution at any particular time enjoys a particular formal authority in virtue of his appointment (e.g., ordination). Of course, in many cases particular specialized knowledge or ability may also be present, but even a "failure" remains in his post. In this sociological configuration superiority and subordination are structural. Formal authority, derived from a current position in the institution, exercises a domination over other members of the group which does not altogether derive from practical necessity.

[4] See the *Staatslexikon*, IV (Freiburg, 1959), col. 325.

In all institutions which may be regarded as institutions in the full sense, formal authority always gives rise to the domination of man by man. There is therefore nothing odd in the fact that the two views mentioned at the beginning of this article should both see a connection between institutions and domination. Whether the form in which domination is exercised is democratic or dictatorial is not without importance, but in either case there is a structure of domination. All attempts to promote fraternity, however well intentioned, stop with official authority. "You are all brethren" (Mt. 23. 8; cf. 23. 10) loses its validity the moment human behaviour is institutionalized. Role authority creates relations of domination, and these cannot do without sanctions. Sanctions are the form taken by social control in institutions. Control ranges from simple warnings to the annihilation of the individual. The form control takes depends on the purposes of the institutionalized community. If an other-worldly salvation is given out as the aim of the group, loss of this "eternal salvation" will be the group's "capital punishment".

Our definition of an institution thus shows that institutions are instruments of power which are normative for behaviour among human beings, even though, or in fact because, they derive from this behaviour.

IV. The "Task" of the Church as an Institution

A group obviously cannot do without general "rules of play", but the exercise of domination ought, in theory, to be avoidable. This is true at least of groups which form as a result of free choice, which one doesn't have to be born into. In the case of the Church, it can be shown from the Bible that a community without domination would be truer to Jesus' idea than an hierarchical institution.[5] In the primitive community, institutional forms were accepted as aids in quite specific emergency situations. It seems to me that Sohm's view cannot be proved either from history or by sociology of religion. It is equally one-sided to describe the Church as an institution based on domination. This is of course historically accurate, but what remains unproven is

[5] G. Hasenhüttl, *Charisma. Ordnunungsprinzip der Kirche* (Freiburg, 1969), pp. 19–70.

its necessity. It is possible for a religious community to renounce the use of domination. It is possible for the Church to renounce power, and indeed as a tendency it is commanded by the message of Jesus. The Church, then, is not described in its essence when it is regarded as an institution, but historically it has regarded itself as an institution and, as a sociological group, it has a certain relation to institutional elements.

If, on the other hand, we look at the question from the other end, and define the Church as the sphere of Christian freedom, it is the Church's task to proclaim this freedom from domination as its basic rule and to institutionalize it in the broad sense (cf. Schelsky's and Metz's suggestions). The Church would then be the institutionalization of freedom from relations of domination and formal authority. In this sense, the term "institution" would acquire a new meaning, since the institution would no longer perpetuate relations of domination but would guarantee freedom from outside pressure. It should not need proving that such an institution on a new principle would make sense, and for evidence that this would be an appropriate role for the Church in society as a whole we may refer to the preaching of Jesus.

How could the Church be turned into the institutionalization of freedom domination (an-archy)?

1. It would have to do without a dogmatic basis laid down by authority. Criticism and self-criticism in open dialogue would be the main rules. All decisions claimed to be final or irrevocable would have to be repeatedly questioned. This is not the result of a desire for relativism or uncertainty whether true knowledge is possible, but an attempt by this method to advance in working out the truth and freely admit mistakes. Any sort of dogmatism would be out of place in such a Church, and every dogma would be subject to revision. Revision means a never-ending readiness to discuss. It means taking Christ as a model and making no claim to absoluteness. This sort of Church would not insist that its view should have precedence and would thereby contribute to the free development of man's understanding of himself. This programme of sympathetic dialogue would be the institutionalization of fredom from domination, embodied in the Church.

2. Ecclesial revisionism follows from an absolute commitment

to freedom and the humanization of life. A Church of this sort would be institutionally tolerant. It would be tolerant among its own members and would refuse to use force in matters of opinion and behaviour. It would practise tolerance to others by not meeting attacks with force, but overcoming evil by good. It would be the model for a non-violent system of community and society. Nor would this tolerance, which did not exclude its own religious institutions from constant questioning, lead to relativism with regard to truth; it would simply be an admission that every view is incomplete.

3. Under this system such a Church would stimulate love of freedom. Institutionalized people, marked from birth by formal authority and so familiar with freedom only in an atrophied form, would first have to be led to the "freedom of the sons of God". Genuine need of freedom would have to be stimulated. In its role as propaganda for Christian freedom, the Church would have to attack all domination as inhuman and ban it from its own structures and institutions. Only when people have lost confidence in the formal, institutionalized exercise of authority can life become more human. The Church could take the first steps in this direction and arouse love of freedom in men's hearts. Its task would be to take away people's fear that without domination and formal authority they would lose their security. Christian freedom is the best weapon against the misuse of freedom. It is true that there can be no guarantee against the misuse of freedom, but is there any against the misuse of authority and power?

4. A Church of this sort, dedicated to spreading the kingdom of freedom or the kingdom of God, would also not be dominated by the principle of achievement usual in society. Where work and drudgery enslave people and destroy them physically and mentally, the Church would leave a space free in which people could breathe. This is the true function of liturgy and worship, and only to the extent that they do this are they truly Christian practices. This would give people free play, an area in which they could really have all the play they wanted. That work and play should coincide, an idea which is inconceivable within the present organization of society, could in such a Church become

the experience of grown, truly mature people. It would not be results that counted. Men would not be admitted on the grounds of their achievement, but their activity would acquire a meaning in itself. The activity of Christians before God has meaning as their working out of their lives, and it needs no confirmation by results.

5. Some people will regard the idea of the Church as the institutionalization of freedom from domination as too good to be true, but why should we not make a start? Did not Jesus Christ, who is "the way, the truth and the life", set us an example by choosing this way?

Or is it really true that authoritarian attitudes cannot be transformed into libertarian ones? Could we not take at least a small step in this direction which would have an effect on the relation between the Church and institutions? Many apostles of freedom have suggested that the public conscience could act as a social corrective. This concept is perhaps too vague to have any real regulative function in a community. If any commandment is to retain its validity for Christians it is the commandment to love. This could be the Church's public conscience. As long as this commandment is limited to the private sphere and only defines a moral category, it can have no social effect. But there is nothing to prevent this commandment to love from itself being institutionalized in the existing Church in order to liberate it from domination and formal authority.

We could start with the existing hierarchical structure, but, as it were, go one better and set a congregation over it, the *congregatio ad fovendam caritatem*, a community for the spreading of love. It would be above the pope, and keep a constant watch on his doctrinal statements and proposals for action. The congregation would have the task of seeing that nothing was done by the hierarchy which conflicted with love. If, for example, an encyclical was against love, the pope would be ordered to revise it. If he refused, it would be published with an appendix containing the congregation's judgment. No office-holder could be a member of this body and half its members would have to be women. This would be one way of dismantling authoritarian structures gradually. Not only the pope, but also all bishops and pastoral clergy would be answerable to such bodies, whose sole task would be to see if anything in sermons, instructions or actions was contrary to love.

A beginning could be made voluntarily by young parish clergy. If they let themselves be guided by such a body, they could avoid the danger of setting up an authoritarian structure based on their position as parish clergy. In such a system control would no longer be exercised through an hierarchical power-structure, but by an attempt to put into practice the principle of love without domination. The Church would then perhaps get a new shape which would be a sign of hope for the world. Have we grounds for hoping for this? It is a hope against hope.

Translated by Francis McDonagh

Gregory Baum

Sociology and Theology

MOST articles dealing with the relationship of sociology and theology are based on presuppositions with which I have considerable
difficulty. They suppose that sociology and theology are unified
sciences, operating out of a clearly defined rationale, and that it
is therefore possible to study their interrelationship in an abstract
manner by comparing and contrasting their respective formal
principles. These presuppositions are present among theologians
who in planning a theological conference request the participation of a sociologist, with the expectation that this one scholar
represents a unified body of truth and a methodology universally
recognized in his science. People often turn to sociologists in the
hope of getting a single answer.

These presuppositions seem to me to be quite unjustified. I
often wonder whether theology itself is in actual fact a science
unified by a single principle. What concerns me in this article,
however, is the problematic unity of sociology. It seems to me
that sociology is a conflictual grouping, within the same university department, of various fields of interest and methodological
approaches, all dealing with society as a human project.

I. VARIOUS FIELDS OF INTEREST

It is easy to mention several fields of interest in sociology that
have special significance for the theologian. There is the sociology
of institutions—I mention this first because the present issue of
Concilium pays special attention to this—which studies institu-

tions and their effect on the people who belong to them and who are served by them. This kind of sociology may be very useful to the ecclesiologist who tries to come to a better understanding of the Christian Church and its institutions. On the more practical side, the sociology of organization may help various ecclesiastical bodies to come to better self-understanding and to see more clearly in which way they must modify their institutional life and activities. Then one could mention the sociology of religion. This vast field of sociological inquiry can be useful for the theologian who wants to come to a better understanding of Christianity and its place in society. What is the social reality of religion? How do the symbols of religion affect men and their society? The applications of the sociology of religion to theology seem endless. Then there is the sociology of knowledge which studies the social grounding of the ideas people have. This special field of study is of great importance for understanding the development of doctrine in the Church and the relation of the various schools of theology to the actual life of the Church. Theologians often tend to regard the variations of doctrines and theology simply as a development of ideas, without paying sufficient attention to the socio-political reality, of which this development is a reflection. The sociology of culture, which studies how the visible environment in which people live has been produced by them, can be of great importance for the theologian who wishes to consult it. For there we learn how the elements that are usually regarded as purely religious are actually cultural factors with great power in the creation of the human environment. Religious symbols, religious vision, religious sentiment are not purely private realities: they actually enter into the project of building the human world. Inwardness, in the eyes of the sociologist, exercises a social function.

These very brief remarks indicate that the relationship of theology to sociology are inevitably complex. For the theologian working in an area of interest in theology—be it biblical, historical, systematic, or whatever—can turn to any field of interest in sociology, enter into conversation with it, and test whether the sociological ideas proposed to him are helpful, within his own theological inquiry, for a better understanding of the gospel and its power in the world. The relationship of theology and sociology, then, is something that must be created. And in creating it many different methodologies are used.

More must be said about the complexity and problematic unity of sociology. Sociology is actually a conflictual field of learning. Several methods and approaches, all of which are represented in sociology departments, are at odds with one another and present different views of human society. These approaches do not constitute various fields of interest within a common body of knowledge; rather, they look upon the study of society from different perspectives. The theologian in dialogue with sociology ought to know, therefore, what kind of sociology he is dealing with. The idea of inviting a sociologist to theological conferences and expecting him to represent a unified, non-conflictual field of study is, as I have already suggested, based on a common misunderstanding of the social sciences.

Since the various approaches adopted in departments of sociology have a variety of theological implications, I shall try, in this article, to give a brief description of the approaches characteristic of North American sociology.[1] This is a risky undertaking, for brief descriptions of complex realities are inevitably schematic and can easily become caricatures. More than that, I am not sure whether my theological sympathy for some approaches may not give a negative taint to my description of the others. Yet I must take this risk: for to be silent about the important conflicts in sociology, in an article on its relationship to theology, would gravely misrepresent the present state of affairs.

II. Conflictual Field of Study

What are the methodological trends found in departments of sociology today? There is first of all the classical sociology, produced by the great scholars of the nineteenth and early twentieth century who created the new branch of knowledge. This approach is occasionally, though quite rarely, adopted by contemporary sociologists. The classical authors are still read and will never be left behind. In them, sociology is close to history and

---

[1] For an initiation into the conflictual field of sociology in North America, see C. Wright Mills, *The Sociological Imagination* (1959), and Robert W. Friedrichs, *A Sociology of Sociology* (1970).

philosophy and constitutes a mode of reflection on, and a systematic analysis of, society, culture and religion as a human project. It is based on the discernment of social patterns and their role in the creation of society. This discernment is corroborated by empirical arguments, though never submitted to a purely quantitative verification. This great tradition (Tocqueville, Marx, Toennies, Durkheim, Weber, Simmel, Pareto, etc.) is so central to the self-understanding of the present society that a lack of acquaintance with it is a serious loss for a theologian or a philosopher.

Classical sociology with its various fields of interests sheds much light on the Christian religion. Since this issue of *Concilium* deals with the Church as institution, let me ask—simply by way of illustration—how a sociologist belonging to this trend would deal with a practical problem posed to him. The example I give should not be understood as an attempt to reduce the application of sociology to the concerns of pastoral theology. If a pastor—this is my example—asked a sociologist in the classical tradition to examine his parish, he would receive a long essay on the history of the parish, which analyses the forces that led to its creation and the cultural influences that have perpetuated it, and spells out the complexities of modern life that make the parish problematic and the special local conditions that may or may not demand a change of policy.

Then there is positivistic-empirical sociology. This trend is characterized by the attempt to assimilate sociology as much as possible to the natural sciences. It is concerned with the quantification and measurement of social action and tries to reach conclusions that are scientifically verifiable. The positivistic sociologist does not feel the need to operate out of a theoretical understanding of society. He thinks that the methods devised by him enable him to be in touch with the facts and draw valid conclusions independent of any theory. He tends to abstract the social action he studies from its historical context: he tries to free his observations from any particular understanding of social development and from any set of values, hoping thereby to achieve scientific results that are more solidly grounded in reality.

If a pastor asks a positivistic sociologist to study his parish, he will receive a wealth of information about the people belonging to the parish and their institutional interaction. But it will be left to the pastor himself to decide how useful this information is and what can be done with it.

Then there are the functionalist sociologists. They operate out of a theoretical understanding of society. They suppose that society is a system of social equilibrium, a common project to which each person and each group make a specific contribution which defines their role in the system. The meaning of social action, then, can only be understood when we discover its place and function in the total social system. Even conflict is appreciated as an element contributing to the balance of the system. Social research, therefore, tries to determine to what extent institutional action is functional and how the institutional elements that are dysfunctional should be changed to make society again the harmonious balance of differentiated roles and offices. Since the functionalists work against the background of a wider theory of society and study social action as part of the total system, it is possible for them to concentrate on very limited areas of social life, on micro-problems, and adopt methods of research that are not very different from those of positivistic-empirical sociology. They, too, strive for strict scientific verification.

If a pastor asks a functionalist sociologist to study his parish, he will get a detailed study of the institution, clarifying the institutional elements that work well and recommending how the institutional elements that do not contribute to the equilibrium of the whole should be modified.

Then there are the critical sociologists. These sociologists do not regard society as a social equilibrium. On the contrary, they hold that there are in society discrepancies and injustices that inflict hardships on people and diminish their humanity. A healthy society, according to the critical sociologists, is a conflictual one, one in which ongoing conflicts between various groups brings to the surface the hidden contradictions and thus lead people to reconstitute their social life. These sociologists are critical of functionalists: for by regarding social equilibrium as the ideal society, they make people look away from present injustices and thus unwittingly protect the existing power structures. Critical sociologists, moreover, are unable to concentrate on micro-problems: for the critical study of a limited area immediately raises wider issues and inevitably leads to an examination of the contradictions implicit in the whole system. Critical sociologists, therefore, have little use for the methods of positivism. They regard the quantification of human life, which this approach presupposes and promotes, as an alienating trend in society. On the other hand, the tendency of critical sociology to relate the limited areas of research to ever wider connections and locate them in the historical development that has produced them, brings it into close proximity to classical sociology, which has always been concerned with wider issues and only looked at micro-problems inasmuch as they shed light on these wider issues.

If a pastor asks a critical sociologist to study his parish, he will get a detailed account of the discrepancies in the parish system and a set of recommendations that will lead, not to peace and harmony, but to the significant conflicts that will raise the consciousness of the people in regard to the contradictions inhibiting their social life. The pastor may even be told that the parish system itself embodies a view of the Church that is no longer in harmony with the self-understanding of Christians and that the problems in the parish can only be solved by abandoning the parish system and by rethinking the Church's mission in society and the manner of organizing the faithful into an effective movement.

Then there is phenomenological sociology. The scholars who adopt this approach are keenly aware that society is an ongoing creation of people who interact through words and gestures to symbolize their common purposes and encourage a common intention. These sociologists doubt whether the kind of empirical observation fostered by the scientific method can come to an understanding of society at all. Society cannot be studied as an object outside of ourselves, apart from our awareness of it. What scholars must do is to make themselves sensitive to what goes on in them and in others as they react to one another and constitute the social process from day to day. Phenomenological sociology wishes to study society not from the outside but by being in touch with the social process from within and clarifying through a systematic methodology what actually goes on in the creation of society. This sociological approach is greatly opposed to positivism. The phenomenological method is able to show how much the quantification of social life, presupposed in much of empirical research, actually distorts the perception of the social reality.

This brief description, fragmentary though it may be, of the conflictual character of sociology makes it clear that the relationship of sociology to theology (or any other branch of knowledge) cannot be defined in a formal way, i.e., on the supposition that sociology is a unified science operating out of a clearly defined rationale.

III. VALUE-FREE AND OBJECTIVE

The conflictual nature of contemporary sociology can be brought out from another perspective, different from the preceding but related to it. I wish to distinguish between a sociology that claims to be value-free and objective and a sociology that claims social research is always and inevitably based on a set of values and on a vision of what life should be like. This conflict rehearses the controversy periodically fought out among social scientists since the last century, regarding the nature of the social sciences. Are the methods used in these sciences the same as those used in the natural sciences? Or is there a significant difference between the sciences dealing with human life and the sciences of nature? May the social and humane sciences imitate the value-neutrality and objectivity of the natural sciences or do they demand a self-critical investigation by which the scientist becomes aware of his own social and personal presuppositions?

The arguments of the sociologists who reject the objective and value-neutral ideal of their science are of great significance and they are not without theological meaning. These sociologists insist, of course, that scholars and researchers must purge themselves of bias and prejudice. In this limited sense, they must seek objectivity. By linking social science to commitment, they do not wish to defend partiality and return to an uncritical pre-Enlightenment attitude towards historical truth. None the less they insist that the claim of objectivity and value-neutrality made by the dominant trend of social science is based on an illusion.

Objective and value-free social science is based on several presuppositions that have been questioned by its opponents. It pre-supposes (1) that the observer or researcher (the subject) and the observed social action (the object) are distinct and separated realities, (2) that the observer comes to a true knowledge of the object to the extent that he detaches himself from his personal values, takes a maximum of objective readings, and draws conclusions from these data by processes that are purely formal and scientific, and (3) that this sort of social science is in no way a political act, i.e., that it is independent of the political views of the researcher and does not favour any one political trend in society.

The sociologists who argue against the claim of value-neutrality and objectivity try to show that these three presuppositions are illusory. They show first of all that the observing subject and the observed object are not completely separated. Why not? Because the same history has produced the observer as well as the social action observed by him. The observer, in his personal history, has come to be through a process which included contact with the object he now studies. For this reason there is an aspect of the object that exists in the observer. Conversely, the object observed has in its historical development been influenced by the observer and his social world. For this reason, there is an aspect of the subject in the object. To suppose, therefore, that subject and object are two wholly distinct realities and that true knowledge is the mental photograph of the object in the mind of the subject is an illusion. What must be undertaken is the difficult task of discovering how object and subject are in fact interrelated, what is their common history, and what is the development of their interaction.

Master and slave appear as distinct and separate. But Hegel has already shown that if the master wants to acquire true knowledge of the slave he must come to greater self-knowledge and discover that he has tied his self-definition to the slave and hence is a slave also. The master must discover to what extent he exists in the other (having made the other slave) and to what extent the other exists in him (having become slave himself by enslaving another).

Related to the first is the second argument that the observer cannot understand the social action he studies, especially if it deals with significant issues, if he is unwilling to change himself. Aloofness may thus prevent him from ever getting at the truth. If the observer has inherited false consciousness about the object of his research, if for reasons of social interest he has disguised the social reality from himself, then the truth will be available to him only as he undergoes a change of consciousness. Here is a radical difference between the natural and the social sciences! To get to the truth of the matter, the natural scientist must refine his instruments; to get to the truth, the social scientist may also have to refine his instruments, but more than that he may have to undergo a transformation of awareness. What is required is a commitment to a human future, in the light of which the present can be evaluated.

Thirdly, the sociologists who argue against objective and value-free social science try to show that the vision of the future and the set of values the observer has adopted affect the angle under which he looks at social action, the questions he asks, the selection of significant data, and the linking together of his findings in the final conclusion. Social science is thus inevitably based on commitment. The scholars who defend the value-free and objective nature of social science have in fact adopted the dominant values of their culture and without intending to do so, actually make their research a confirmation of the given social structure. If this analysis is correct, then the claim of value-neutrality and objectivity is an illusion which disguises a deep cultural and social conformism. Even the determined effort of the scholar to be unpolitical does not enable him to separate himself completely from his vision of what tomorrow should be like. The "is" and the "ought" are never totally separable in human experience. What is necessary, therefore, is that the social scientist become as conscious as possible of the values implicit in his social research and assume responsibility for his vision of human life.

These critical scholars advocate a new ideal of objectivity in social research, an ideal that on the one hand enables them to overcome bias and prejudice and on the other makes them aware that the truthful assessment of the social reality is possible only for persons committed to the humanization of man. Objectivity in this perspectival sense implies the readiness to be freed from the levels of false consciousness implicit in culture and society.

Social science, then, ceases to be a mere description of the social reality; it becomes a manner of perceiving society that leads to its transformation.

IV. Conclusion

These remarks confirm that the theologian cannot turn to sociology supposing that it is a unified science. Instead he must acquaint himself sufficiently with the various trends and the significant controversies in sociology and possibly make his own choice, following principles drawn from his *theological* understanding of the human world, with what kind of sociology he wants to enter into dialogue. The conclusion, then, of this article is that the relationship of theology to sociology is something that must be created. It is not a given to be analysed (given by the very nature of the two sciences), but a multiple project to be undertaken. The theologian must engage in creative theological work through which the sociological understanding of the human reality is made to shed light on the Christian message regarding sin and salvation.

Gérard Wackenheim

Ecclesiology and Sociology

AT THE present time, in colloquia and symposia on the subject of the Church, theologians are very ready to listen to what sociologists have to say. They are quite clearly waiting for something: a sociological illumination, as is sometimes said. It is true that their expectations are often not gratified, either because the sociologist's analysis appears too facile or too pretentious to the theologian sensitive to the mystery of the Church, or because, finding themselves powerless to discover any common area in their dialogue, they both fail to elaborate their viewpoints or even to formulate their questions in terms of the two disciplines. None the less the difficulties of dialogue and the disappointments which may result from it should not be allowed to obscure the fact that a collaboration has at least begun and that this corresponds to the wishes of a good number of theologians. This fact is significant.

The fact is itself evidence of a certain ecclesiology. The appeal to the sociologist presupposes in fact a lively awareness of the Church's situation in society and a conception of the Church as a society of men (*ex hominibus*, while being in principle *de Trinitate*) which, as such, is a proper subject for sociology. Indeed two sociologies normally develop in relation to the two main points of this ecclesiological awareness. Before defining them, it is worth emphasizing their common denominator as well as their novelty. In both cases, attention is concentrated on the ecclesial reality, considered on its own or in its relations with the world. It is no longer a question of religious sociology holding forth upon the essence of religion, nor of a sociography describing religious requirements. It is rather a sociology of the Church and, more precisely, a sociology of a particular Church.

I. The Social Conditioning of the Church and the Ecclesial Conditioning of Society

Any given Church constitutes in general a sufficiently active, coherent and original group for the question of its relationship with society to be a meaningful one. Apart from a period of confusion in the ninth and tenth centuries when, as much from the point of view of the *autoritas sacrata pontificum* as from that of the *regalis potestas*, the *ecclesia* was considered as identical with Christian society, the Church regards itself and is regarded as a more or less important group in society. That is to say that the ecclesial group and the global society are not indifferent to one another, either in fact or in intention.

The fact becomes clear when one considers that the members of the Church are equally members of society and that the latter surrounds and penetrates the Church at all points. The intention existing on both sides also leaves no room for doubt—the Church wants to be open to all and recognizes that people belong to it in many different ways. It sees the roles fulfilled by itself and society as reciprocal (cf. *Lumen Gentium*, 13; *Gaudium et Spes*, 40–45). For its part, society grants the Church a more or less legitimate place and welcomes, tolerates or challenges its role.

Since the Church is a group within society, the question of its relationship presents the sociologist with a preliminary field of investigation which is extremely vast and the relationship between the two powers constitutes only a small sector of this. The investigation as a whole has sometimes been and is sometimes still conducted in terms of "conditioning". This implies an attempt to discover how the organization and the culture of the Church have been conditioned by the society around it. It is said, for example, that it was contact with the Roman Empire which prompted the Church to make the law the privileged tool of its unity. (This is, however, not true to the same extent of the Eastern Church, although it has a longer history of coexistence with the Empire.) It has also been said that Thomas Aquinas was able to

write so extensively on the society of the angels simply by copy-
ing the classifications and attributes of the Roman functionaries
sent by the emperor.

Short of deliberately bowing to an assumption which is deter-
minist, economico-technical, demographic or political, it is essential to take the opposite perspective and ask oneself to what extent
certain structural and cultural elements of society are to be found
in the dependence of the Church, its institutions and its doctrine. History is not lacking in examples of initiatives taken by the
Church and subsequently adopted by society or even imitated
immediately in the sphere of hospitals, education, administration
and law, as well as the influence exercised by religious values on
the future of society, for instance, the influence of Calvinist ethics
on the evolution of Western capitalism.

Today observers ask, and not ironically, if the Church "in
crisis" is not the laboratory which offers the greatest chance of
innovation in terms of communal life, modes of authority and
participation. In certain countries it is certainly not difficult to be
a pioneer in these matters, since society as a whole gives evidence
of great conservatism, in spite of the affirmation of new principles or even the promulgation of reformist texts. It goes without saying that the doctrine and the structures of the Church, as
well as the experiments which are taking place within it, can
act as a brake as well as a driving force as far as social change is
concerned.

The above examples are intended simply to demonstrate that
there is just as much reason to question the ecclesial conditioning
of society as that of the social conditioning of the Church. This
is necessary so long as the Church is not simply accepted as a
belated reflection of society. Even if the Church does give this
impression at certain periods, the facts seen as a whole forbid
such a simplification. It would, moreover, be surprising theoretically if a group which has lasted so long should be without any
substance or route of its own, even if only by reason of its
history.

To examine the relationships between Church and society in
terms solely of conditioning represents a fairly crude approach,
an initial stage. The study has to be taken further and a real
analysis must take place, starting from first impressions which

are concerned in particular with the reciprocity and interaction of influences. To do this, it is necessary to analyse the concepts of the Church and society in detail, to distinguish the relatively simple elements on both sides, to become aware of the correlations between the elements of the two worlds. It is also appropriate to achieve a balance between the elements—those which seem to have most weight are known as independent variables, those which appear to have no exceptional influence will be called dependent variables. It is also convenient to find a balance within the independent variables in order to recognize the "conditions" which facilitate or block any modification of the dependent variables and the factors which exert a stronger and more direct action on the latter. All these comparative studies—which can be described by the expression "functional analysis"—often lead to a better understanding, that is, to a more precise and more sensitive understanding of the liaison between ecclesial and social phenomena. Unfortunately the techniques used for this purpose by sociology at the moment are more and more difficult to apply the further one travels up the macro-sociological ladder, because of the growing complexity of situations and the difficulty of obtaining the information needed rapidly.

The above remarks are well illustrated by a classic sociological example and by the most recent researches. In his study of suicide Durkheim establishes that Protestants commit suicide more than Catholics and Catholics more than Jews. A simplistic conclusion would be that, in relation to the dependent variable suicide, one of the independent variables is likely to be religious faith. Durkheim is wary of such a conclusion, since cross-checking with other facts—single people commit suicide more often than married, married people without children more often than married people with children—brings an awareness that it is the relatively weak integration of the groups to which the suicide belongs which is in reality the cause. He concludes that suicide varies in inverse ratio to the degree of integration of the social groups of which the individual is a part. As far as religions are concerned, therefore, the independent variable in the sense of a facilitating condition is not faith itself, but the psycho-social nature and the level of cohesion of the ecclesial groups in their day-to-day life.

The recent researches which I would like to quote as my

second example bear on the relationship between ecclesial and electoral behaviour among French Catholics. (The situation to be analysed is not perhaps that of the most recent years, but this is less important.) Drawing on statistical results concerning both voting and religious practice, in particular attendance at Sunday Mass in rural cantons of thirty-six departments, it can be stated that the sectors where the right and the centre-right receive a high proportion of votes are also those where religious practice is high, and inversely there is a negative correlation between a left-wing vote and religious practice. The results do not, however, enable us to conclude that the people who go to Mass and who vote for the right wing are the same people.

Research is therefore orientated towards other facts—statements by individuals gathered by sample investigations instead of behaviour numerically assessed. In this case it appears that political preference ties up most clearly with religious attitude, and not with other variables such as sex, profession and age. But is this a direct link, or have the two sorts of behaviour, political and religious, a common dependence in relation to a third variable? For example, might not the two types of behaviour both depend on the socio-professional category? Socio-professional class clearly gives rise to nuances, but the primary link is not placed in doubt in any way. What is more interesting is the discovery that the sectors where this correlation is strong form regional blocs: the West of France, south of the Massif Central, one part of the North, the East and the North-East. Might it not be in these conditions the region itself, in the sense of a common culture forged by history, which might play the role of a third variable in relation to politics and religion and which would constitute the extrinsic link between the two? In other words, might not one explanation of the correlation in question be explained by the fact that electoral behaviour and religious practice are found within the same regional culture?

This explanation merits examination, but it has to be admitted that, for the moment and in France, the region as an historico-cultural phenomenon remains a hypothesis. In looking at the line of indications produced by the polls, one begins to ask oneself if there is not perhaps some intrinsic link. Would not the various types of influence which the Church has on the conduct of the believer give rise to a sort of orthopraxis, a certain internal coherence of behaviour and attitudes? And in the case of others, where the above correlation is not found to be verified, is it not inevitable to suppose a different ideological structure?

The interest in undertaking research such as this is in showing how one can be led to consider groups of factors and even to postulate functional wholes. In this last case, one sometimes passes from functional analysis to a "functionalist theory" of culture and society. In this way religion and the ecclesial reality tend to be explained in their historical position by the function or functions that they fulfil, or inversely by their dysfunctional and very debatable position in a given socio-cultural environment. These views well illustrate the fact which was our starting-point in this first section, to find out the situation or incarnation of the Church in society. They also allow the Christian to understand how and why his group is leaven and light in the world.

II. A SOCIOLOGY FOR ECCLESIOLOGY; AN ECCLESIOLOGY FOR SOCIOLOGY

Sociologists are interested in the Church as a group, in its structuring and its functioning, in its values and models of behaviour, in its expressions and its symbolism in the widest sense. This is the second psycho-sociological type of sociology of the Church mentioned in the introduction.

The field is enormous. Among the sectors investigated are objectives, activities and devolution of roles, the conception and exercise of authority, teaching (including its content and functions), the strata and hierarchies, the organized bodies and the less formal groups, organization and institution, the network of ecclesial relationships, information and public opinion, the modalities of ecclesial relationships (collaboration, competition, lethargy, conflict), the dynamics of church life, the centres of initiative and processes of change, unity and diversity, means and material conditions and relations with the world and the attitude of the world towards the Church.

These sectors are at the moment not all investigated to the same extent by sociologists. This does not mean that they have not already been the subject of some study. Christians, in particular theologians in such matters as the history of institutions, canon law and pastoral theology, certainly did not have to wait for the development of sociology before beginning to know their Church. Sometimes they have been preoccupied with justifying it theologically. Sometimes they have been anxious to criticize and reform it. The advent of sociology has, however, produced innovation, not just because of its techniques of investigation, but more fundamentally because of its method. Like any other group, the Church is seen, as K. Lewin puts it, as an interdependent entity (which integrates with history and the social environment) and any explanation of one sector or of one phenomenon must be made in terms of this interdependent entity. The Catholic theologian would perhaps be content, in order to justify the emergence of the papacy in Rome, to mention Jesus' words to Peter and Peter's arrival and martyrdom in Rome.

Without rejecting these facts, the sociologist would widen his researches and ask other questions: why Rome and not Antioch, and why was papal power defined as it was? He would formulate explanatory hypotheses: the status of the city of Rome within the Empire, its position as a cross-roads, the decadence of the Empire and of imperial authority in the West or the need in a certain cultural context for a central authority in order to preserve unity (similar services were asked of the Christian emperors themselves while they had authority). Not all these hypotheses are worth retaining and are not all equally valuable, but the sociological method implies that they should be used.

It can be seen from what has been said that the sociology of the Church is in no way opposed to ecclesiology. It is carried on with those who live within the Church and who know about it. Only it does not limit itself to this one source. All the same, the sociology of any organization is unthinkable if the views of those who who work in it are not taken seriously into account and all the documentation which can be provided by the organization is not assembled. In addition, however, it is necessary to use direct observation, to collect outside information and above all to attempt a proper sociological explanation.

It is desirable that the Church should respond to the sociologist's expectations by stating what it is and how it sees itself. It speaks of itself frequently in biblical or symbolic terms. This is its undeniable right. But some working definitions are required for the sociologist to choose that which best fits in with the object of his research. When it is, for example, a question of an inquiry into an ecclesial group (parish, diocese or national Church) what limits to set is regularly a problem. How is the Church to be delimited, what criteria can be used? Who is part of it, and who is not? Lacking any precise directions, the inquiry runs the risk of starting badly or, in mistaken prudence, concentrating on the hard centres of the group—the permanent people, the hierarchy—reinforcing the idea of a Church identified with its cell-groups and of an ecclesial life reduced to movement and communication in a descending order. The conciliar texts clearly draw on another and rich source (cf. among others *Lumen Gentium*, 1–17), but the sociologist simply draws from this the concepts that he needs. In any case these texts were not designed for such a use.

Just as a certain ecclesiology is needed for sociology, it is right that there should be a sociology which answers the needs of ecclesiology. Vatican II has given a prominent place to the themes of co-responsibility, co-operation and participation by the people of God in their life and mission. In order to realize these objectives, the sociologist is in a position to point out ways and conditions. Experience teaches him that participation presupposes information and that information is inseparable from a certain delegation of power. How could someone take part in an action with generosity and imagination if the relative facts escape him? How could the information be spread if the person possessing it did not agree to share his knowledge, that is, share too the possibility of intervention which knowledge permits? Anyone who has knowledge can give his authoritative opinion and put forward an appropriate solution; by the very act of doing so, he shares to a certain extent in power. The sociologist who hears participation in a group extolled will have two comments to make. He will say first that anyone who genuinely wants the end will find the means and will go on to say that participation is one of a group of interrelated realities, that is, information, a certain distribution of power (the degree of which has to be decided) and participation. Without this, there is only idle speculation, unless the group under consideration is not really a society of men and so, in consequence, the usual laws do not apply to it. Many other ways in which sociology would be able to be of help to ecclesiology might be quoted, but I think that the formula "a sociology for an ecclesiology" is sufficiently clear.

There remains one other meeting-point and field for collaboration between the two disciplines which should be mentioned. Whether it is a question of sociology or ecclesiology, it is above all a "-logy", that is, a discussion of a social reality. Each of the two sciences, starting from its own inspiration, could point out to the other implications which are perhaps hidden and unsuspected by its own discussion. Sociology is, for instance, in a position to give this help to ecclesiology in connection with the concept of the "body" as an analogy of society.

This is a very ancient analogy. We find it first in the mouth of a Roman senator, Menenius Agrippa, who round about 500 B.C. tried to convince the people to put an end to a secession at a moment when Rome was under attack by external enemies. He told the people assembled on the sacred hill the fable of the man whose limbs refused to give food to the stomach in order to punish it, as a result of which, deprived of nourishment themselves, they died too with the organ on which they had wished to avenge themselves. Subsequently the analogy of the organs was taken up, perhaps rediscovered, utilized by many authors including, among the most well known, Aristotle, St Paul, St Thomas, Herbert Spencer and Pius XII.

The tradition here is both sociological and ecclesiological. In ecclesiology the adjective "mystical" has been applied to the body since the twelfth century. "The Church as the mystical body of Christ" is a term which received the blessing of Vatican II, as did the concept of "organism" which describes the Church from its visible, external aspect. In sociological language the image of the body is intended to underline the unity of a group. But it denotes a rather intense solidarity, in which conflict is unthinkable, implying at the same time a strict and definitive hierarchical system (the stomach will never become the body, and the body will never become the feet). If in coining this image, one argues from it in relation to existing situations, one ends up with an excellent means of justifying peace at all costs, the *status quo*, and privileges. History and sociology both provide evidence of this. It is not wrong for the theologian to be aware of this, so that, in his discussion of the problems, the *unum corpus* remains *sub uno capite* which is Christ himself.

Drawing on its inspiration and experience, ecclesiology can for its part encourage semantic clarity on the part of sociology, so preventing its becoming a philosophy, which is either deliberately or unconsciously unaware of what it really is.

Translated by Rosaleen Ockenden

PART II
SOCIOLOGICAL ORIENTATIONS

Niklas Luhmann

Institutionalized Religion in the Perspective of Functional Sociology

METHODOLOGICAL discussions within the branch of sociology known as functionalism seem today to be in a state of stagnation. Since it was discovered that functional analysis went no further than a comparison in relation to particular problems, the methodological problem has turned into a theoretical one, into the question of the origin of these "problems". The systems theory is an attempt to answer this question.

I. The Differentiation of Social Systems

In sociology, the theory of social systems deals with complexes of significant actions whose significance is both their unifying principle and what marks them off from their environment. Since all human activity can ultimately be understood in terms of a general meaning of the world, the formation of social systems depends on the existence of specific dominant attitudes which separate out identifiable sub-systems. These attitudes may be places where people live or meet, goals worked for together for a period or a history experienced in common. Only a few of such attitudes which have influenced system formation have become important for society as a whole, or indeed in their own later development.

The evolution of human society can be regarded as a process of increasing differentiation of social systems, and in the first place as the development of a uniquely social and specifically human system of society. Thomas Luckmann has well said that

45

this requires a "desocialization" of the world. The emergence from this process of differentiation of particular systems of society for specifically social and interhuman relationships makes possible within these societies the increasing formation of func-- tion-specific systems for the various fields of politics, domestic family life, the economy, the legal system, religion, science, and so on. This makes society as a whole more complex and more efficient in its subsidiary functions, and as such structural development becomes less probable there is an increase in the number of problems to be solved and in the system's liability to disturbance, though the possibilities of substitution also increase at all levels of system formation.

Functionalism regards itself, in terms of its object, as historical and evolutionary, in the sense that in all individual analyses it must presuppose a differentiation of systems, each with its particular problems. A functional sociology of religion or sociology of the Church is also concerned with a contingent object, the existence of which is the only basis for its analysis. This radical attitude to contingency gives traditions of demystifying criticism of religion points of contact with a number of theological views of the content of faith.

II. The Function of the Religious System

In this approach religion is not defined in terms of the existing objects of belief, as it were by finding a general concept to cover any possible content of faith, such as "belief in supernatural entities". Nor is it defined by particular qualities of feeling or experience. From the point of view of functionalism, religion is the manner in which a specific function is performed under conditions which may be changed by evolution. What is this specific function of religion?

All attempts to give a direct answer to this question have failed. They have proved either too narrow or too comprehensive, or, as in discussions of the integrating function of religion, have made both mistakes at once. One way out of this difficulty is to combine functionalist methods with a systems theory which takes account of evolution. This approach allows, and indeed requires, an analysis at a number of levels. A general function, not specific to religion, must be postulated and a more precise analysis then made of how sub-systems of society are differentiated and on what sets of problems they concentrate.

Any postulate of a general meaning can be derived from the general theory of social systems as constitutive of meaning.[1] It depends on the fact that, when any meaning is formed, either on the level of perception or on the level of thought, a surplus of possibilities is produced on which the moral conscience must operate selectively. *Complexity* is the term used to indicate the range of these possibilities, and *contingency* that which describes the fact that all reality is modally given as a possibility which might have been different.[2] The formation of any society depends first of all on a transformation of undefined complexity and contingency into defined or at least definable—in other words, on a definition of the world or at least a guarantee of its definability. This is not just a justification of choices already made, an explanation of events which have taken place, a vindication of the immediate situation. A more important function of this definition, or guarantee of definability, is that it at least offers a possibility of increasing complexity and contingency and so making tolerable a higher degree of uncertainty and insecurity.

This general function is performed in every society, and is the basis of meaningful choice in experience and action. Until modern times it was performed by underlying assumptions which we normally describe as religion.[3] The performance of this

[1] On this, cf. N. Luhmann, "Sinn als Grundbegriff der Soziologie", in J. Habermas and N. Luhmann, *Theorie der Gesellschaft oder Sozialtechnologie—Was leistet die Systemforschung?* (Frankfurt, 1971), pp. 25-100; *idem*, "Religiöse Dogmatik und gesellschaftliche Evolution", in K.-W. Dahm, N. Luhmann and D. Stoodt, *Religion—System und Sozialisation* (Darmstadt and Neuwied, 1972), pp. 15-132.

[2] The scholastics also talked of the *complexio contingens*, but at the same time retained the concept of the world as the *universitas rerum*. An attempt to conceive of the world itself as *complexio contingens* means abandoning this conception of the world as an *aggregate* and imagining it as a correlate of systems which constitute meaning. There are attempts at this in Husserl which, however, are not developed.

[3] This description is not based on a clear concept of religion covering specific phenomena. This is deliberate, since the question to be answered is how far, and to what types of society, religion as a distinct phenomenon describable in itself can be attributed. Being cultural heirs of the world religions, we perhaps tend to apply this concept too widely to primitive and archaic social systems.

central social function was identical with the role of religion in society, and changed with that role. In a variety of forms, religion provided the assumptions about the world and bases of interpretation which enabled its definability to be subordinated to moral conduct. Within this general function a variety of subsidiary functions may be distinguished as required: the justification of moral values and claims, the absorption of collective and individual fear, the control of *rites de passage* and ambiguities, etc.

As a religious system becomes differentiated during the historical evolution of a society, and becomes institutionalized as a separate system distinct from politics, the economy, the armed forces, the law and the family, the conditions under which this function is performed alter. This is what is meant by "institutionalized religion" in the title of this article. Differentiation does not mean that religion shakes off social ties, becomes independent or self-supporting and exists without social connections. No social system can cut itself off in this way from the social network, unless it becomes a separate society.[4] Differentiation means, rather, that religion must reconstitute itself on the basis of membership of and non-identity with society. There are various forms or levels of solution to this problem, such as the immediate exchange of food for religious benefits or the level of ecclesiastical organization with particular obligations connected with entry and retention of membership.[5] The social forms of this differentiation also determine the way in which the non-identity of religion and society (and its individual aspects, religion and the family, religion and politics, religion and the economy, religion and science) is reflected within the religious

[4] This point can be very well demonstrated in cases of religious inspired emigration, as in the settlement of North America.

[5] Cf., for example, S. J. Tambiah, "The Ideology of Merit and the Social Correlates of Buddhism in a Thai Village", in E. R. Leach (ed.), *Dialectic in Practical Religion* (London and New York, 1968), pp. 41–121, or G. Condominas, "Notes sur le bouddhisme populaire en milieu rural de Lao", *Archives de sociologie des religions*, 25 (1968), pp. 81–110, 26 (1968), pp. 111–150.

For a good explanation of the novelty of the organizational solution to the problem of differentiation, see A. D. Nock, *Conversion* (London, 1961). Directly related to this are the construction of particular "creeds", the effort to distinguish between orthodoxy and heresy and the accompanying stimulus to the formation of a theological system.

system. The social forms determine, for example, whether a society's religion merely offers the possibility of earning particular merits or religious benefits, whether it makes a claim to regulate social life, or whether it restricts itself to channelling goodwill into subsidiary services.

III. Higher Toleration of Indeterminacy and Complexity

These ideas can be further developed by the use of material from ethnology, comparative religion and sociology of religion, but we have no space for this here. Instead we shall discuss the more theoretical question of the meaning and possible consequences of the transfer of a central social function, such as the transformation of undefined into defined or at least definable complexity, to a specialized sub-system. How can the sort of direction which is important to any meaningful life at any period be communicated to particular situations, roles, places, occasions, values and dogmas when it has been separated out into an independent technique?

If we start, with Malinowski and others, from the concept of human needs, it might be supposed that religious needs are much like other needs. Everyone must be adequately fed, but there is no need, nor is it possible, to eat incessantly. Systems theory uses more abstract analytical tools to reach findings which take us a good deal further than such slick answers.

As a main thesis we may suggest that the differentiation of the function of defining the undefined increases the performance of that function in a particular direction. It increases it by generalizing and specifying possibilities of a specifically religious direction, the level of contingency, complexity and uncertainty tolerable in society as a whole, in relation both to the world and to the society itself. The classical example is the certainty of the existence of one God, which makes it possible to give a religious interpretation of the political and economic disasters of one's own people. Abstraction from the tribal god to the world God makes God compatible with good and bad fortune and even with good and bad behaviour. This remains true even if at the same time one has to aim for political successes and prevent political setbacks within the society, to try for economic profits and avoid losses.

Another example: the dogma of original sin and the postponement of reward make it possible to live with the fact that even one's brothers in the faith sin (perhaps even more than the heathen) and that one shares the sacrament with people who may be damned. Such generalizations do not lead, at least not at first, to simple tolerance. They produce a higher level of combined security and insecurity, and this is their significance for the development of more complex societies. They make religion compatible with more than one state of society, and enable it to perform its specific function in relative independence of its context and of changes in other areas of society.

This formulation, based on Hebrew and early Christian religion, also received impressive confirmation in the Reformation period. The problem here is concentrated in the question of the certainty of faith, which was paradoxically resolved by making certainty follow directly from the intensity of fear and uncertainty. Similarly the most external foundation of faith on Scripture alone was in fact the most internal.[6] The incorporation of such paradoxes into the justification of faith (or, more accurately, into the reflexive justification of faith by faith) made faith unshakable in precisely the sense that it became compatible with any possible world and any possible society.

An adequate understanding of such models is impossible if one connects them with the satisfaction of religious needs as though these were constants existing prior to all religious institutions or dogmas. Nor do they serve the function of supporting a society's attitudes or its processes of domination and distribution[7] All of this is their inevitable accompaniment in the sense that there are general social restrictions on religious speculation and indoctrination—just as one tends to fall in love within one's own social class, just as economic restrictions on research, political restrictions on the economy, etc., are unavoidable. Apart from this, however, what is remarkable is that the emergence of a distinct religious system makes possible a code of belief which

[6] For this, see K. Heim, *Das Gewissheitsproblem in der systematischen Theologie bis zu Schleiermacher* (Leipzig, 1911), esp. pp. 220 ff.; P. Althaus, *Die Prinzipien der aristotelischen Scholastik* (Leipzig, 1914), esp. pp. 179 ff.

[7] The functional equivalent of this in the area of practical moral theology is moral casuistry, which in its confessional practice developed both probabilism or laxism and a strong emphasis on social compatibility.

prepared the way for modern society by its indeterminacies, paradoxes, positive-historical basis and defensive symbols (e.g., "interiority" as a symbol of defence against social, paradoxes as a symbol of defence against logical, controls). The religious system —at least in its formal theology, if not as a popular religion—produced the level of structural indeterminacy and unique complexity which was a necessary condition for further social evolution. It did this, moreover, before the transition to bourgeois society had got under way in economics and politics.

IV. Higher Toleration of Insecurity and Contingency

The same process of increasing generalization and specification of the structure of the religious system, and in particular of its dogmas, can also be analysed in terms of systems theory in connection with the problem of contingency. Our initial premise was that religion performs the social function of transforming undefined contingency into definable. With the emergence of a separate religious system specializing in this, a specialized mechanism now becomes available for this, namely the transformation of external contingency into internal. Everything in the world can change; the unexpected is always possible. Death stands unnoticed at the door. In this situation religion says that everything happens in accordance with God's will, the contingency of which is at least capable of meaningful interpretation; it may be fearful in wrath or inexhaustible in mercy, but it is never spiteful or arbitrary.[8]

In this way the problem of contingency is reformulated in terms internal to the religious system, and this provides easier points of contact for further treatment. Which points are used depends in each case on the switching mechanism which makes the transformation possible. For monotheistic religions the formula for contingency is contained within the concept of God himself. God is all-powerful; he can, without being checked in

[8] On the beginnings of a religious contingency which was, as it were, morally and logically domesticated, and on its connection with a (no longer archaic) monotheism, see M. David, *Les dieux et le destin en Babylonie* (Paris, 1949). As regards the social structure the basis of this was the non-identity between the High God and the ruler, i.e., in a differentiation of roles between religion and politics.

any way, always be different. Given this, the world and every-thing he has created is always contingent in a sort of supra-modal necessity. A different and potentially atheistic version is *karma*, the all-embracing cosmic mechanism which regulates everything that happens according to merit and guilt. In both cases contingency is understood as "dependence on", which is itself a re-formulation of the prior problem of different possibilities. In both cases also the structural indeterminacy and the interpretative freedom of the religious system are acquired by leaving the origin of the chains of dependence in the unknown. God's will is un-fathomable and the conditioning of *karma* by a previous life cannot be remembered because death and birth extinguish memory. Both versions of the problem of contingency also make possible a (centralized or decentralized) localization of the prob-lem of contingency in the form of a ground with regard to which interpretations can develop relations. In this way a combination of structure and indeterminacy is produced which fits in with the co-operative and interpretative potential of priestly roles. In this version the problem can be taken over on to the level of roles and translated into the details of the day-to-day adminis-tration of contingency.

This analysis has shown that very different dogmatic construc-tions can perform the same function and to that extent be func-tionally equivalent. This does not mean that they have the same results. Quite the opposite—*karma* and God presumably differ enormously in their power of abstraction, their power to provide motivations and offer comfort, and above all in the degree of centralization they require in the religious system. It will be seen from this how important the choice of a religious system is in these respects, even though, from an evolutionary viewpoint, they may have come into existence more or less haphazardly.

One of the most productive lines of inquiry in this connection is to ask whether, and under what conditions, the problem of contingency itself may become explicit in a religious system. Nor-mally it is left in code. This is a requirement of its function in transformation and also of its use in the code of the communica-tion medium of faith. In spite of this, medieval theology brought the problem, together with all its logical complications, to con-sciousness. The contingency of the world became a corollary of the concept of God, and the contingency of religious doctrines themselves became irrefutable in view of their basis in revelation as an historically localizable event.[9] With its paradoxical proclamation of deepest uncertainty as firmest certainty, the Reformation also led to the decoding of contingency. At this point, however, it was shown that the religious system as a whole could choose not to follow theology's pressure for reflection.[10] There are evidently in the infrastructure of the religious system independent problems and functional requirements which do not automatically give way to the analytic achievements of a highly developed theology.

V. THE INSTITUTIONALIZATION OF RELIGION

The problem of the ability of dogmatic systems to control the religious system even in such matters as official actions and the practice of good works is also part of our study of institutionalized religion. Here, exceptionally,[11] I use the concept of insti-

[9] This connection really requires closer analysis. One of the aspects to be taken into account would be the change in the view of time which first made the character of revelation as an event into a problem. It made the present a point and thereby destroyed the possibility of seeing an historical event as ever-present.

[10] Of particular interest to the sociologist are the effects on ecclesiastical politics of different views of the problem of contingency. For an example from the famous debating topic *de futuris contingentibus*, see L. Baudry, *La querelle des futurs contingents (Louvain 1465–1475)* (Paris, 1950). Another disputed topic in theology and religious politics, the reason for the incarnation, similarly involved an interpretation of contingency, in the question whether the incarnation was a free self-revelation of God or should be regarded as conditioned by the fall and directed towards salvation. Cf. A. Spindler, *Cur verbum caro factum?* (Paderborn, 1938). The subject is treated variously, either mainly in terms of the God contingency formula or mainly in terms of the motivation mechanism of faith. I would see the sociological content of the controversy in this, and not, with A. M. Knoll, *Zins und Gnade* (Neuwied and Berlin, 1967), pp. 5 ff., in differences between "class theologies". Knoll rightly sees that one of the points at issue was the primacy of a framework taking in the world as a whole as opposed to a view confined to the Church, i.e., where the emphasis in the transformation of contingency should be placed.

[11] For my normal use of the term, see N. Luhmann, "Institutionalisierung: Funktion und Mechanismus im sozialen System der Gesellschaft", in H. Schelsky (ed.), *Zur Theorie der Institution* (Düsseldorf, 1970), pp. 27–41. I departed from this practice in an attempt to do justice to the subject I was given.

tutionalization in Talcott Parsons' sense, to describe the integration of various levels of a system's structure.[12] The dominant structures of a social system (for Parsons values, for us and in what
follows contingency formulas and dogmatic systems) are institutionalized to the extent that they can be successfully translated
on to the level of behaviour patterns, roles and collectively binding
specific actions. If they cannot be so translated, they remain
decoration or ideology, selectively quoted and taken into use from
below as immediate needs require.

A necessary condition for this problem to arise at all is a level
of differentiation and development of the religious system which
is seldom reached. The religious system must be differentiated not
only on the obvious level of visibly sacral, ritual action, but also
on the level of interpretations of meaning. In other words, it
must have developed a special view of the world as a whole
and be capable of communicating it. A dogmatic system may
then arise to control and co-ordinate these interpretations which
sanctifies particular concepts, key interpretations and combina-
tions of ideas, and at the same time, by generalizing them, gives
them sufficient flexibility to deal with events in the world, its
own texts and religious experiences. An independent need for
strongly systematized direction and decision then arises at this
higher level of the dogmatic system. Efforts to meet this need
cannot, however, be developed to the full, since this is only one
of the problems a religious system has to solve. They must take
account of, and are limited by, the demands of other levels of the
system.

The level which is concerned with providing interpretations
of immediate relevance to the outside world presents its own
non-dogmatic problems. These include the ability to give answers,
plausibility, ability to adapt to situations and deal with those involved in them. Religious ideas are required here mainly in the
form of proverbs, suitable texts and examples. In particular situations problems of dogmatic consistency can often be neglected,

[12] Perhaps the best introduction is L. H. Mayhew, "Action, Theory and
Action Research", *Social Problems* 15 (1968), pp. 420–32, esp. pp. 422 ff.
See also Mayhew, *Law and Equal Opportunity* (Cambridge, Mass., 1968),
esp. pp. 9 ff., for a study in the sociology of law which has parallels with
the following.

especially when there is no counter-argument. The difficulties of dogmatic control increase with the differentiation of the system and the need of the public for interpretation, and finding a solution to this problem becomes more and more urgent as the religious system abandons ritual and shifts its impact on its environment to the provision of interpretations.

In moral casuistry an attempt was made to solve the problem of different levels by deliberate incongruity and by maintaining secrecy about practical advice. This way presupposes the discipline of a religious order, and in addition has problems of legitimation which make it difficult to transfer to the religious system as a whole. This means that the problem of differentiation and integration of several levels of symbolic generalization remains open. It appears that the Churches have so far not seen this problem as a stimulus to systematic investigation or dogmatic analysis, but have relied on secondary mechanisms, either organizational, like hierarchical centralism or pressure to unite in communities or teams, or training. Neither of these supports can be overworked, and they are now showing signs of overloading. The limits of official pronouncements from the centre on dogmatic questions are clear. The custom of training the young in a dogmatic system, socializing them in the Church and then leaving them to their own resources[13] limits the ability of the dogmatic system to react to the change of generations and turns the problem into one of generation conflict. These solutions to our problem of co-ordination and integration are also now showing signs of strain. In this situation a valuable question which functional sociology could ask institutionalized religion is whether there may not be untapped possibilities in dogmatic theology which could carry out the transformations of undefined into defined or at least definable possibilities in a more convincing manner for our generation.

Translated by Francis McDonagh

---

[13] Learning theory gives general support to this way of using time differentiation of stages of life to embody a differentiation of levels. Cf. J. M. Scandura, "Role of Rules in Behavior. Toward an Operational Definition of What (Rule) is Learned", *Psychological Review*, 77 (1970), pp. 516–33.

Rudolf Siebert

Religion in the Perspective of Critical Sociology

IT IS our purpose to explore the theory of religion produced by the critical sociology of the Frankfurt School. This critical theory of religion can only be understood in the context of the fundamental structure of critical sociology. This structure needs first to be clarified. Against this structure as background, the main aspects of the critical theory of religion will then be discussed.

I. THE FRANKFURT SCHOOL

The critical sociology—or the critical theory of societal process —has been developed by Max Horkheimer in co-operation with Theodor W. Adorno, Herbert Marcuse, Erich Fromm and others in the Institute for Social Research in Frankfurt am Main, Germany—the so-called Frankfurt School. The evolution of the critical sociology in the Institute is richly documented in the *Zeitschrift für Sozialforschung*, edited by Horkheimer from 1932 to 1940.

The critical sociology has come to its fullest bloom so far in the immensely prolific literary productivity of the Frankfurt School after it was re-built by Horkheimer and Adorno in the University of Frankfurt in 1946. Some of the most outstanding publications of the Frankfurt Institute in the last quarter of a century reach from Horkheimer's and Adorno's initial co-operative work, *Dialectics of Enlightenment*, to Horkheimer's *Concerning the Critique of Instrumental Reason*, Adorno's *Negative Dialectics*, Marcuse's *Counter-Revolution and Revolt*, Fromm's

Revolution of Hope, and Habermas' *Knowledge and Human Interests*.[1]

Few philosophers and sociologists have resisted so persistently and heroically all fascist temptations of late civil or bourgeois society during the last fifty years as those of the Frankfurt School. There existed in the nineteen-thirties and forties not only a Confessing Church, but also a confessing group of intellectuals in the Frankfurt Institute for Social Research. Unlike the resistance of the Confessing Church against fascism, that of the critical sociologists was not motivated by faith but by autonomous reason; not by revelation but by enlightenment. Fascist counter-revolutions have in common that they all regress behind the Freudian enlightenment of the twentieth century, the Marxism enlightenment of the nineteenth century, and even the Encyclopedists' enlightenment of the eighteenth century. The Frankfurt School integrates all three waves of enlightenment in its critical theory of societal process. At the same time, the critical sociologists are aware of the dialectics of enlightenment—the shadow it throws; its inner limitation; its affinity to the guillotine; its tendency to turn over into its opposite—rebarbarization. Under social conditions pointing to rebarbarization, critical sociologists continue to promote enlightenment: to help men and women in late civil or bourgeois society to conquer their fears and to become masters of their fate. A deep passion for enlightenment characterizes the attitude of critical theorists to society, seen as essentially a pro-

[1] The description of the structure of the critical sociology is based on: M. Horkheimer, *Zeitschrift für Sozialforschung*, 1932–1940 (Munich, 1958); M. Horkheimer and T. W. Adorno, *Dialektik der Aufklärung* (Frankfurt, 1961); M. Horkheimer, *Zur Kritik der instrumentellen Vernunft* (Frankfurt, 1967); T. W. Adorno, *Negative Dialektik* (Frankfurt, 1966); H. Marcuse, *Counter-Revolution and Revolt* (Boston, 1972); E. Fromm, *The Revolution of Hope* (New York, 1968); J. Habermas, *Knowledge and Human Interests* (Boston, 1971); T. W. Adorno, *Ästhetische Theorie* (Frankfurt, 1970); M. Horkheimer, *Vernunft und Selbsterhaltung* (Frankfurt, 1970); H. Marcuse, *An Essay on Liberation* (Boston, 1969); E. Fromm, *Escape from Freedom* (New York, 1968); H. Marcuse, *Eros and Civilization* (New York, 1962); T. W. Adorno and Others, *The Authoritarian Personality* (New York, 1969); H. Mayer, "Nachdenken über Adorno", *Frankfurter Hefte*, 25 (1970), H.4, pp. 268–80; T. W. Adorno, "Über Mahler", *Frankfurter Hefte*, 15 (1960), H.9, pp. 643–53; T. W. Adorno, "Die Soziologen und die Wirklichkeit", *Frankfurter Hefte*, 7 (1952), H.8, pp. 585–95.

duction-and-exchange process, as well as to its superstructure—
art, philosophy, science, and also religion.

II. INDIVIDUAL AND SOCIETY

Like all other styles of sociology developed in the last hundred
and fifty years in Europe and America, the critical theory is
essentially concerned with the relation between the individual
and the collective. Yet critical sociology is unique because of its
method of negative, historical dialectics, developed by Horkheimer since 1931.

Unlike other types of sociology, critical theory does not hold
on to the fixed dualism of individual and society, nor does it
reduce it monistically in terms of an abstract—and therefore untrue—individualism or collectivism. It rather resolves such dualism dialectically. Individual and society are separate but also inseparable. They reproduce each other. They can only be
understood through each other.

Critical or dialectical sociology is philosophical in orientation.
But it never shies away from the hard work of detailed empirical
research. Where civil or socialistic society continues the mimesis
of nature, natural science methods are in order also in the critical
theory—as in functionalism or behaviourism. Yet critical
sociologists tend to focus on specific areas of empirical research—
personality, family, production, exchange, ideology, prejudice,
music, and also religious institutions—in the context of the dialectical movement of the individual and the collective. In this
dialectics alone, social and cultural facts reveal their inner meaning to the critical theorist.

Critical sociologists broaden the sociological concepts of individual and society continually into the philosophical categories
of the particular and the universal. Those categories constitute
the core of the critical theory. They are taken from Hegel's
dialectical *Logic*. The identity of the particular and the universal
constitutes Hegel's "notion of the notion"—the peak of his *Logic*.
The historical roots of both categories go deep into the philosophy and theology of the Middle Ages and antiquity. The
"effort of the notion" is the *nervus rerum* of the critical sociology
as of Hegel's philosophy. But while Hegel stressed the identity

of the particular and the universal, the critical theorists emphasize their non-identity. Their dialectics is as negative as that of Hegel was positive.

According to the analysis of critical sociology, late civil (or bourgeois) society is fundamentally characterized by a radical dichotomy between the particular and the universal. On one hand we have the atomized, isolated anomic individual and, on the other hand, a society tending—for this very reason—towards total administration or totalitarianism. The individual, frightened by loneliness, disorientation and helplessness, is only too willing to escape his merely formal freedom and to capitulate before and give support to the all-powerful collective, which degrades him. The authoritarian personality abandons himself to the false identity of the particular and the universal—so characteristic for the fascist state.

The critical sociologist traces, by the power of his negative dialectics, the decline of the individual in Western civilization to the very limit of the subjectless, totally regimented society. What is threatened by this type of society is exactly that which biblical religion introduced into Western civilization—the principle of the independent person, his subjective freedom, his infinite value, his salvation as an individual and not only as a species, his subjectivity or selfness, not selfishness. This principle underlies Christianity as well as enlightenment. At this time the powerless particular is forgotten in the all-powerful universal. The critical theorist is extremely cautious with regard to a possible future restoration of a more concrete individual in a more rational society in terms of a positive dialectics. Negative dialectics is intended by the critical sociologist to prevent the transformation of the utopia of concrete subjectivity, mediated by community, into an ideology for the justification of the existing orders of domination. Only in the extreme *aporia* of the complete loss of the individual in the entirely administered society appears to the critical sociologist a glimmer of hope against all hope— the resurrection of the individual in body and soul in a future, more humane society.

The thinking of the Frankfurt School is emphatically anti-positivistic and essentially utopian. Dialectical sociology refuses to be nothing else than the duplication in thought of the given social reality. It is not value-free as the positive social sciences allegedly are. Its utopia and its highest value are the free society. The free society is one in which the particular and the universal, the individual and the collective, the private good and the common good have been reconciled.

No matter how far the critical sociologist carries the negativity of his dialectics—and he does so to an heroic extent—it never touches his utopia of the reconciled society. It is here that the critical sociologist becomes affirmative: he is negative only because of this ultimate affirmation.

Dialectical sociology is critical not only in the sense that it clarifies fundamental concepts which are, in late civil society, in the process of losing their meaning—like reason, freedom, justice, love, tenderness, truth. It is fundamentally critical by putting all social and cultural phenomena under the criterion of the utopia of the true homeostasis of the particular and the universal. As long as only one or a few are free in modern societies, on the basis of the ownership of the means of production, to make economic as well as political, military and cultural decisions for the many who are the mere objects of their manipulation, the tragic estrangement between the particular and the universal prevails. The domination of the many by the despotism of the one or the few, via the silent controls hidden in production and exchange, is the cause for the antagonism or even indifference between the particular and the universal in late civil society. They will be reconciled only when all are free.

The Frankfurt School's categorical imperative is the achievement of the emancipation and the solidarity of humanity, the freedom of all, the reconciliation of the individual and society, the universal individual, the total man. This categorical imperative is for the critical sociologist the criterion by which he measures human behaviour in the sphere of society as well as in the sphere of art, philosophy, science, and not least of all, in religious institutions.

III. CHALLENGE AND RESPONSE

The critical theory of religion contained in the dialectical sociology of the Frankfurt School continues and in many ways concludes the critique of religion, which Kant and Hegel initiated at an earlier stage in the development of civil society. The critical theory of religion has been developed particularly on the basis of, as well as against, Hegel's *Philosophy of Religion*. It has further been inspired by A. Schopenhauer and F. Nietzsche, by Karl Marx and Sigmund Freud, not to forget De Sade.

The thinkers of the Frankfurt School, particularly Horkheimer, Adorno and Marcuse, are familiar with the theological tradition of antiquity, the Middle Ages and modern time—from Tertullian, Origen and Augustine, via Thomas Aquinas and Duns Scotus to Pascal and Kierkegaard. Critical sociologists have developed their theory of positive religion throughout the last forty-two years in continual contact with Christian thinkers like Theodor Haecker and Jacques Maritain, Theodor Steinbüchel and Romano Guardini, Josef Pieper and Otto von Nell-Breuning, Paul Tillich and Reinhold Niebuhr, Walter Dirks and Eugen Kogon, Karl Barth and Karl Rahner. Even in the mid-nineteen-twenties, Adorno and other members of the later Frankfurt School were in dialogue not only with great Jewish but also with outstanding Catholic and Protestant theologians in the circle of the so-called "Great Frankfurters", including Martin Buber, Ernst Michel and Paul Tillich. For Horkheimer, Paul Tillich remained always the model of a good, loving Christian.

Despite all of these contacts, the critical theory of religion was developed completely on the side of enlightenment and in opposition to religion in general and Christianity in particular.[2] It challenges all religious traditions and institutions. In 1958, a dialogue took place in the University of Münster between the Christian thinkers Dirks and Kogon and the emphatically non-Christian Adorno on the theme of "Revelation and Autonomous Reason". They agreed to disagree. While Dirks and Kogon pleaded for a new encounter and a possible reconciliation between

---

[2] Concerning the structure of the critical theory of religion see above (note 1); in addition, see: T. W. Adorno and E. Kogon, "Offenbarung oder autonome Vernunft", *Frankfurter Hefte*, 13 (1958), H.6, pp. 392–402; H.7, pp. 484–98; M. Horkheimer, *Kritische Theorie* (Frankfurt, 1968), pp 361–76; W. Dirks, "Am Schnittpunkt", *Frankfurter Hefte*, 24 (1969), H.9, p. 618; H. Marcuse, "Marxism and the New Humanity: An Unfinished Revolution", in J. C. Raines and T. Dean (eds.), *Marxism and Radical Revolution* (Philadelphia, 1970), pp. 3–5.

faith and reason, revelation and enlightenment, Adorno argued the point that enlightenment had already since the eighteenth century superseded Christianity. But he did not therefore exclude the possibility of co-operation between critical sociologists and reflective Christians. Dirks and Kogon, editors of the Christian *Frankfurter Hefte* and Horkheimer and Adorno, directors of the Frankfurt Institute, co-operated with one another—as believers not bound to petrified orthodoxies and men of enlightenment not enslaved by a shallow enlightenment-ideology—in intellectual distance as well as with mutual respect and trust.

A new Averroism is at hand in the form of the critical sociology, including its theory of religion. A new *Summa Contra Gentiles* may very well be desirable in the Christian community as response to the challenge of the new radical, sophisticated, progressive naturalism—the *error perennis* in the *philosophia perennis*—of the Frankfurt School, which comes to its peak in its theory of religion. The work of Dirks and Kogon and their friends in and around the *Frankfurter Hefte* throughout the last thirty years as well as the new political theology constitute the beginning of a positive Christian response to the very wholesome challenge of the Frankfurt School.

IV. SOCIETY AND RELIGION

The core of the critical theory of religion is the dialectical relation between society, state and history on one hand, and the relig ous superstructure on the other hand. Dialectical sociology is, like all enlightenment, *reductio ad hominem* of all social and cultural phenomena, religion included. Like all materialistic—empirical, historical, naturalistic—theories of religion since the Hellenistic enlightenment, the critical theory considers God to be a product of human feeling—of the fear, joy, hope, helplessness, selfishness, or the longings for goodness, justice, love of individuals and groups. The God-concept has no objectivity in and for itself. The result is atheism.

According to the critical sociologist, what has been preserved in the God-concept is the conviction that there exists another, higher measure of human thought and action than that expressed in nature and society—namely God as absolute goodness, justice or love.[3] The religious acknowledgment of a supreme, all-powerful and at the same time absolutely good and loving being received its strongest energies from the people's discontent with their fate in nature, the sphere of inequality, and in repressive formations of society. People hypostatized and absolutized as eternal goodness, justice and love the harmony of the particular and the universal which they were deprived of in social orders of domination. The deeper the estrangement between the individual and society grows within a certain state, the greater becomes the longing of its people for the eternal reconciliation of the particular and the universal in "heaven"; or also the desperation or even indifference concerning it. Both happened in the evolution of civil society, recently the latter more often than the former. Hegel and Mark had noted at a much earlier developmental stage of civil society that it deprives the masses even of the consolation of religion.

In the perspective of the critical theory of religion, Christianity has been for too long not negative, that is, not critical enough. Far too often, particularly in the Constantinian part of its history, Christianity has failed to present the ideals of goodness, justice and love to an unjust society and state. It preferred to side positively with the establishment. It invested with the aura of heavenly justice the unjust masters of society, thereby legitimizing them and giving the many a reason for sacrificing themselves willingly and humbly for the few in the production process as well as on the battlefields. Christianity lost its eschatological salt and became an ideology justifying the establishment. It thereby only intensified the dichotomy between the particular and the universal and prevented their reconciliation in a freer society. In a word, it became reactionary.

According to the dialectical sociology, religion is only too often concerned more with its exchange-value for the powerful few in civil society than with its own absolute truth-value. Even late civil or bourgeois society may still consider religion to be necessary, but this necessity is not the inner necessity of the absolute truth of religion. It is rather an external necessity. Civil society must, like any earlier formation of society, fulfil the functional

[3] Horkheimer, *Kritische Theorie, op. cit.,* p. 374.

requirement of integration in order to survive. Parsonian functionalism reflects this. Civil society uses religion as an integrative, equilibrating, stabilizing factor—as band-aid for the social system's victims, who otherwise could possibly rebel. To be religious in civil society saves men from communism: but whether one believes in the absolute truth of religion or not does not seem to matter. Bourgeois materialism is equally indifferent to the subjective spirit of man, the objective spirit of society or the absolute spirit of religion. In reality, the functional necessity of religion for late civil or bourgeois society is conditional and this means contingent. Religion is necessary only for the integration and the survival of civil society, if the latter does not decide to substitute it by another mechanism—moves, football, the state—which fulfils the same task which religion did before and may do so even more effectively. Critical sociologists observe that religion becomes more and more dispensable as an ideology in industrial society. After the inner necessity of the absolute truth of religion had already vanished during the eighteenth and nineteenth centuries, today even its external functional necessity becomes more and more doubtful.

The critical sociologist is horrified by the ambiguity of Christianity as well as other positive religions. In 1933, Karl Barth wrote his *Theological Existence Today* and *For Freedom of the Gospel*, which were directed against National Socialism. But in the same year, Hans Michael Müller wrote *The Inner Way of the German Church* and *What Must the World Know about Germany? National Revolution and Church* in favour of National Socialism. Both theologians based their arguments on the Bible. Millions of Christians died for, as well as against, fascism. Christianity motivated people to love their neighbours or even their enemies among racial, ethnic, cultural or religious minorities. But it also produced dangerous prejudices among masses of people and incited them to pogroms, witch hunts and participation in holy inquisitions. There has existed for centuries an authoritarian Christianity which supports all the reactionary trends of its time.[4] But critical sociologists also find in history a libertarian Christianity—Christian humanists, Brothers of the Free Spirit, the

[4] Marcuse, "Marxism and the New Humanity: An Unfinished Revolution", *op. cit.*, pp. 9–10.

Edomites, men like Martin Luther King, Camilo Torres, the Ber-
rigans, Helder Camara—which has supported the historical trend
towards autonomy and solidarity. Critical sociologists feel sympathy for Christians of the libertarian mould. Critical theorists
suggest to men and women of religion to reflect upon the dialectics of religion—its shadow, its inner limitation—as they ad-
monish themselves and other men and women of enlightenment
to be aware of the dialectics of enlightenment, so that inhuman
effects of enlightenment as well as of religion be eliminated.

Concerning the future, the critical sociologists, following their
negative dialectics, predict the end of religion in a completely
secularized society with little chance for a restoration in a more
concrete and truer form in a just society. The limits of negative
dialectics become visible in the critical theory of religion as no-
where else. Hegel may still be right after all—only the unity of
negative *and* positive dialectics, analytical understanding *and* syn-
thetical reason, leads to the full truth. There is, nevertheless, a
trace of positive dialectics present in the critical theory of religion.
The content of religion—absolute truth, goodness, justice, love—
will be restored in a relative and finite form in the social and
political practice of the reconciled society. The form of religion
will be abandoned. In the future free society, in which the true
identity of the particular and the universal has become reality,
men and women will be able, according to the critical theorist,
to live without religious myths and by finite but nevertheless
autonomous reason alone. In the reconciled society, the age-old
religious promises of happiness will be fulfilled, as much as this
is possible by men and women who have found out that they are
for themselves and on their own in the universe.

V. Utopia and Eschatology

The critical sociologist pleads for a political utopia as opposed
to a religious eschatology. Utopia is the key to enlightenment
and its core is finite, earthly happiness. Eschatology is the key to
religion and its core is infinite, heavenly happiness. The critical
theorist of religion is certain that the great eschatological dream
of eternal happiness found, in one form or the other, in all positive religions, cannot be realized. The prayers of the persecuted

and the innocent who must die without clarification of their cause, do not reach their goal: no divinity intervenes in their favour. Auschwitz—and all the inhumanity of history it stands for—is, to the critical sociologists, the proof of atheism. The night of history which the light of autonomous human reason does not elucidate, is not penetrated either by the light of absolute Divine Reason. There is no God, no absolute will or providence to whom the oppressed could direct their prayers. The eschatology of eternal happiness has as little ground as absolute truth or infinite love. That this is monstrous does not mean that it is not true. Monstrosity has, in the eyes of the critical sociologists, never been a valid argument against the assertion or denial of any state of affairs. Logic does not contain the law that a judgment would be false, if its consequence was desperation—at least not negative, dialectical logic.

The critical sociologists understand fully the eschatological wish for the appearance of universal justice and goodness and infinite happiness. But their analysis of society, state and history lead them only to a feeling of infinite abandonment and loneliness. A metaphysical melancholy can be found in the writings of critical sociologists as in the works of all great materialists. They nevertheless consider their feeling of infinite, metaphysical loneliness the only true answer to the impossible eschatological hope of religious man for ultimate happiness.

Beyond that, the critical sociologists replace the eschatology of infinite happiness by the utopia of finite happiness. They are deeply concerned with the transformation of the social and historical reality principle in favour of the emancipation of the pleasure principle. The pleasure principle will be fully realized in the future non-repressive society, in which the particular will no longer be sacrificed to the universal. The absence of repression is for critical sociologists the prototype of freedom *and* happiness.

The critical theorists hold that pleasure carries within it the consciousness of its transitoriness and the bitterness of its end. The humanistic protest of critical theorists throughout the last forty-two years against the unnecessarily and senselessly diminished life of the majority of men has its origin in this experience of the irretrievability of human happiness. The critical theorists find an affinity between hedonistic utopia and actual historical partiality for the sufferings of the oppressed and degraded in history, an affinity they do not acknowledge for religious eschatology.

Critical sociologists are realistic enough to see that the realization of the concrete utopia may remove the societal but not the natural ground for men's melancholy. The cruel and bitter negativity of death remains. But according to the critical theorists, death will change its face after the competitive civil society, in which everybody is at war with everybody else and with the whole society, will have been transformed into a just society, where there is a balance between individual and common interests. In the free society, death will be stripped of all religious euphemisms and ideologies. Deideologized death will infinitely strengthen the solidarity of all men and women against death. For the critical theorists, the religious eschatology of the new heaven and the new earth to be created after the destruction of the old world goes one step too far in its assault on the melancholy of human existence. The real utopia of the free society, which will not only tolerate but enhance the full realization of the physical and spiritual potential of each individual, negates what the critical sociologists consider to be the illusionary character of religious eschatology, but it preserves the truth it contains—man's wish for and right to happiness.

VI. Reconciliation

Critical sociology including its theory of religion represents Western enlightenment at its best in today's world, at a time, that is, when most people are more inclined to underestimate than to absolutize the power of human reason. Critical theorists do not only radicalize the dichotomy between individual and society, but also between society and religion, free world consciousness and faith, utopia and eschatology. These forms of dichotomy are interconnected. Is there a chance of reconciliation, we ask, between enlightenment and religion, so that both may serve the future reconciliation of the particular and the universal in the free society?

Hegel rightly observed that if the dichotomy between enlight-

enment and religion has once come into existence, it will necessarily lead to despair if it is not settled through knowledge, and
we may add through social practice. This despair takes the place
of the unachieved reconciliation.[5] Some of this despair we find
in the Frankfurt School, despite its hopeful orientation to the
concrete utopia of the reconciled society. Adorno's students observed in the eyes and gestures of their teacher an expression of
deep sadness, anxiety and horror concerning the senescence process of Western civilization during the last months before his
death in 1969.[6]

Critical theorists agree that there cannot be a double truth. But
it is also not possible to reduce the truth of religion to that of
enlightenment or vice versa. Simply to eliminate one of the two
sides has never led to real inner peace, neither in the earlier Hellenistic nor in the modern Western enlightenment.

It seems that the Frankfurt School precisely by radicalizing the
dichotomy between religion and enlightenment, faith and autonomous reason, has brought into the open the necessity for their
reconciliation. It is necessary if our civilization should no longer
be put into question merely negatively, but for our salvation's
sake, positively towards more humane goals.[7] Could it not be—if
we may be allowed to engage in utopian thinking and positive
dialectics for a moment—that with the beginning of the reconciled society, people would also become free enough to develop
new forms of a more concrete and truer enlightenment as well
as forms of religion, for which the infinite would appear in the
finite and the finite in the infinite.[8] That was the core of Hegel's
reconciliation programme in his *Philosophy of Religion*.

This programme has not become entirely obsolete, it may even
have gained in relevance by the continual deepening of the gulf
between individual and collective, society and religion in the last
century and a half. Each of them—the finite and the infinite—
would no longer constitute a separate sphere—a godless social

[5] G. W. F. Hegel, *Vorlesungen über die Philosophie der Religion* (Stuttgart–Bad Cannstatt, 1965).

[6] Mayer, "Nachdenken über Adorno", *op. cit.*, p. 280.

[7] Adorno and Kogon, "Offenbarung oder autonome Vernunft", *op. cit.*,
H.6., p. 397.

[8] Hegel, *Vorles ungen über die Philosophie der Religion, op. cit.*, p. 34.

world and a worldless God. Neither would there be a regression towards a natural—or social—pantheistic fusion of both. It is certainly not entirely unthinkable and impossible that a new formation of society would come about, in which faith in the God, who makes "all things new" (Apoc. 21. 5), could be reconciled with the type of knowledge and intelligence no longer concerned (merely positivistically) with the given and the old but with such "new things". Such a reconciliation must, of course, correspond to the highest demands of knowledge. Reason cannot and should not sacrifice anything of its dignity. On the other hand, such reconciliation must also do justice to the absolute truth-content of religion which must not be drawn into the finite dimension. Theology cannot be entirely reduced to anthropology, psychology or sociology. The absolute content of religion, the wholly other, the absolute non-identity, must be respected by the finite form of knowledge. Only such respect can, in the last analysis, protect enlightenment from its tendency to turn over into its opposite—rebarbarization and enslavement of the many by the few or by the one.

Critical sociologists hesitate usually to identify what they may possibly have in common with reflective Christians in the present world historical situation, despite the obvious divergence of their intellectual positions. But Adorno, the great philosopher, musician, sociologist, and a deeply humane man, did once formulate in what reflective Christians and critical sociologists, men of enlightenment, do indeed converge: Both care and demand that, in all seriousness, no man in this world should **any** longer be hungry; that there should no longer be any wars; that no man should any longer be sent to a concentration camp.[9] In those practical demands, the solidarity of reflective Christians and critical sociologists presents itself, despite all differences, much clearer and stronger than in all the so-called theoretical positions they may take concerning society, family, personality, state, history, art or religion. In this solidarity, they have co-operated in the past and can and will continue to do so also in the future towards the realization of the reconciled society, in which all will be free.

[9] Adorno and Kogon, "Offenbarung oder autonome Vernunft", *op. cit.*, H.7, p. 498.

Franz-Xaver Kaufmann

The Church as a
Religious Organization

NEITHER the everyday nor the sociological use of the word "organization" is sufficiently precise to make the subject of this essay clear in advance. By "organization", as used of a social phenomenon, may be understood the totality of its structural characteristics, its particular character as a purposive entity, directed towards a goal, or a particular, formalized structure of sets of human actions. The particular meaning presupposed in the term "organization" is therefore crucial in determining what is discussed—or ignored—by a treatment of the historical phenomenon "Church" or "churches" under this title.

This article is not concerned with a discussion of concepts, but it is still necessary to make our starting-point clear. We start from the assumption that the social organization of the Western churches has changed in the course of their historical development in the direction of a higher degree of formal organization as understood by recent organization theory. We shall claim that this change of organizational form has particular consequences for the way in which members of the Church perceive the Church, and correspondingly for their religious motivations. We shall try to show that this changed relation between the individual and the institution is the result of general developments in society, and not primarily an internal process within the Church. This raises the question as to what changes in the Church's view of itself are necessary to enable it to reach an adequate understanding of the problems mentioned here.

I

Almost insuperable difficulties stand in the way of a sociological reconstruction of early Christianity. We have some basic data. The appointment of the Twelve (Mk. 3. 13–19; Lk. 6. 12–16) and of the seven deacons (Acts 6. 1–6) may be seen as indications of a structure among the followers of Christ and in the original Jerusalem community. The overwhelmingly local character of the early Church is also clear, as is the development of two principles of leadership, collective leadership by the elders (probably the heads of Christian families), a presbyteral system and leadership by an individual appointed for the purpose, episcopal government. However, since these two organizational principles seem to have been involved in the first dispute between Jewish and Hellenistic Christians, none of the interpretations of the organization of Christianity which derive from the Christian tradition can be regarded as purely objective. This is even truer of later interpretations of the organization of the primitive Church. The Catholic tradition in particular emphasized all the factors which seemed to legitimate the actual development of the Catholic Church, especially the supra-local unity of "the Church" and its hierarchical structure, which were claimed to have existed from the beginning. On the other hand, the Protestant tradition seems to us to restrict the transition from a primitive charismatic community to an institutionally organized Church to too short a period. A knowledge of sociology would incline us to presume that the social organization of Christianity drew on existing models of social organization, although the selection from among the various models available was governed by the rapidly developing Christian tradition.

A sociological reconstruction of the social organization of Christendom would also have to bear in mind that historical interest, in the sense of investigation of the actual social forms of Christianity and their development, did not come into being until the nineteenth century, more or less at the same time as the periodization and structuring of Western history by historicism. The theoretical interests of the history of Christianity were at least in part determined by the situation of Christianity at the time, i.e., by its social embodiment in churches which were in fact just beginning, in that century, to see themselves as separate social structures. The discussion of the separation of Church and State, which was the main issue in religious policy in the nine-teenth century, should be seen as a symptom of the process of structural and functional differentiation of society which took place with increasing speed from the beginning of the modern period. This process has, of course, led to the present situation of the freedom of the Church and institutional religion in many respects from political, economic and other social ties, and to the corresponding freeing of these areas from religious connections. Secularization and the structural differentiation of society must be seen as complementary processes.

This situation, in which the churches had acquired a social form, gave historical interest in the history of Christianity its direction. The history of Christianity came to be seen as the his-tory of the Church, and quite often as the history of the historian's own Church. And what counted as "church" in this context was determined by the modern view of the Church; it was the task of history to trace the roots of this in the past. Church history became, for the Catholic Church in particular, a legitima-tion of its own identity in the present. One sign of this was the tendentious use of the marks of the Church as empirical charac-teristics at the First Vatican Council, and another is the close connection which continued into this country, between the theo-logical disciplines of Church history and apologetics.

II

This Church-centred interest in the history of Christianity led to various limitations, of which the following are the most im-portant for our subject.

1. The definition of the Church as the "official" Church, i.e., from the particular viewpoint of its professional organizers. This meant in practice that the Church was for the most part identi-fied with the clergy, and in the process the changes in the social characteristics of the clergy in the course of history were neglected. A consequence of this limited view was that all the forms of religious organization which did not have an "official"

character tended to be neglected in the description of the Church as a religious organization.

2. The definition of "office" exclusively as hierarchical office. "Office" and "Church" became central concepts by which the Church's view of its own organization was given theological expression. This led to a view of church organization which ignored even those phenomena within the "Church of the clergy" which cannot be easily reconciled with the hierarchical principle. Examples are religious orders and the growing area of administrative posts.

This narrow self-definition has organizational consequences which emerge, particularly at present, as problems.

1. In the face of a decline in vocations and a simultaneous growth in organizational requirements, the identification of "office" with clerical status has led to the appearance within the formal organization of the Church of forms of organization which cannot be justified theologically. Sooner or later this may be expected to produce considerable tension.

2. The hierarchical principle presupposes one-dimensional relations of authority and subordination, but this organizational principle is hardly any longer adequate to deal with the new and very complex problems produced by modern organizations. Nevertheless, since they wish to retain this principle on theological grounds, the hierarchy attempt to make the Church's real organization conform to it. This may be suggested as the reason for the tenacious insistence on the territorial principle in church organization. It is only within a territorial—or, in Durkheim's sense, "segmentary"—organization that the principle of leadership by means of one-dimensional authority and subordination can be consistently applied. There is therefore a connection between a theological view of office and and opposition to functional forms of organization in the Church. The principle of structural and functional differentiation, which is today characteristic of almost all areas of society, is rejected on theological grounds.

It will now be seen that the problem is not a simple one of the continuance of church structures which developed and proved valuable in the feudal social structure which preceded the emergence of bourgeois society. The organizational backwardness of the Church is not simply a problem of cultural lag. It is much more than that and involves questions of the Church's self-definition which need to be examined with the techniques of the sociology of knowledge and the organization theory.

A sociological consideration of the organizational aspects of the Church reveals very clearly a difficulty which faces any consideration of social macro-structures. These institutions have a view of themselves which the sociologist cannot accept without examination, because this view normally fails to include all the phenomena which the objective observer would have to ascribe to the institution. Indeed, to reveal latent aspects or functions of an institution is one of the main practical functions of sociology. In our view, however, it is not possible to abstract completely from the view the institution under examination holds of itself and produce a definition exclusively on the basis of sociological theory. In spite of the vagueness of their boundaries, social macro-structures do have an historical identity which is in fact determined by their view of themselves. This does not, however, exclude the possibility of a change in their sociological characteristics.

If this view of the situation is right, the main importance for the churches themselves in the present of a sociological consideration of the concept of the Church derives mainly from the fact that the traditional understanding of the Church can no longer be reconciled with the changes in the social forms of the Church and Christianity. This in itself is not a new phenomenon. What is new is that the organization of the Church has much more importance now than in the past for the transmission of Christianity. This is why organizational problems can now no longer be covered by the veil of theology.

III

Although our intention is to create an awareness of the problems of churches as organizations, our study is not conducted primarily in terms of organization theory, but aims at a theory of the way in which Church and religion are constituted in and by society.[1] In our view, the attempts to gain recognition for this

---

[1] Even when social studies of the Church go beyond investigations of

dimension, made in the past by Max Weber and Ernst Troeltsch, are the most important work in contemporary sociology of religion. As against descriptions heavily dominated by theory, we would wish to insist, with Weber and Troeltsch, on the need for an approach guided by the history of Christianity.[2] For a mediation of sociological and theological attitudes, at least, this approach seems to us essential.

Weber and Troeltsch regarded the Church as a particular social form of religion, and especially of Christianity. "Church" is taken as a term for an institutional type of religious organization.

The "Church" is distinguished from the "sect" in the sociological sense of this word in that it regards itself as the administrator of a sort of entail of the goods of eternal salvation which are offered to all. One does not normally join the Church voluntarily, like an association, but one is born into it, and the non-religious person is subject to its discipline just as much as the religious. In short, the Church regards itself, not, like the sect, as a community of persons qualified by a personal charism, but as the bearer and administrator of a charism of *office*.[3]

The distinction between personal qualification and office as a structural principle of social organization is not limited to the Church type, but is a characteristic of all bureaucratic organizations. Indeed, in Weber's description the organizational form represented by the Church appears as the historical prototype of all present forms of bureaucratic organization.

---

the "simple faithful" to deal with the more delicate problems of church organization, there remains the danger that they will uncritically accept the Church's own interpretations of the problems or themselves adopt too specific theories and concepts—e.g., from the sociology of organization—in the description of the problems. In our view the approach based on organization sociology must always be supplemented by that of the sociology of knowledge, since organizational and ideological elements are fused in the Church in a way unparalleled in any other type of contemporary organization.

[2] I have in mind in particular the writings of Peter L. Berger, especially *The Sacred Canopy* (Garden City, N.J., 1967), and Niklas Luhmann, especially "Religiöse Dogmatik und gesellschaftliche Evolution", in K. W. Dahm, N. Luhmann, D. Stoodt, *Religion—System und Socialization* (Darmstadt and Neuwied, 1972), pp. 15-132.

[3] Max Weber, *Wirtschaft und Gesellschaft, Studienausgabe* (Cologne and Berlin, 1964), 2. Halbband, p. 880; also E. Troeltsch, *The Social Teaching of the Christian Churches* (London, 1931).

Against Weber, it may be claimed that this institutional "Church" type is the product of a development in the historical Church which lasted into modern times. It is certainly true that the first attempts to give the constitution of the Church legal form can be traced back to Tertullian and even, in a sense, to Irenaeus' teaching on the law and tradition,[4] and these laid the intellectual foundations for the later organizational development. This is a ground for seeing later institutional forms as the working out of a principle which can be traced back to the early period of Christianity. The development of a "professional bureaucracy" in Weber's sense, i.e., the development of the priesthood into a profession, took place very gradually at first and, in the Catholic Church, did not reach its decisive stage until the post-Tridentine reform of priestly training and the introduction of the obligation of residence for priests and bishops. It was also in the post-Tridentine period that the decisive transition to a bureaucratization of the Catholic Church occurred, with Sixtus V's reform of the Curia, which abolished the share in the government of the Church which the college of cardinals had enjoyed since the Middle Ages. It was not until this time that the cardinals became top Vatican officials. Although the structural principles of the institutional Church were by this time fully developed, their practical application was not completed until the nineteenth century, after many setbacks in the intervening period.

In the Protestant churches the development of the institutional principle and of bureaucratization was most advanced where the Church was a state Church. It will be seen from these remarks that that contrast between "Church" and "sect", in spite of the apparently historical basis of the typology, encourages an unhistorical view of social forms of religion. Nor is a refinement of the typology enough to deal with the present problems. What is required for this is an approach which enables us to account for the origin of and changes in organizational forms of religion which see themselves as having always existed in their present form.[5]

---

[4] Cf. R. Hernegger, *Macht ohne Auftrag. Die Entstehung der Staats- und Volkskirche* (Olten and Freiburg, 1963), pp. 81 ff.

[5] For details see J. Matthes, *Kirche und Gesellschaft. Einführung in die Religionssozziologie*, II (Reinbek–Hamburg, 1969), esp. pp. 110 ff.

IV

If we are examining the Church from a sociological point of view as a "religious organization", the premises of our examination must be made clear.

1. Christianity has from its beginning been realized in various social forms. The range of these forms has been determined both by the history of Christianity and by the social conditions existing in the various periods.

2. The struggle to find the correct form of Christian existence does not take place just on the level of faith, ideas and creeds, but simultaneously on the level of social organization, and especially through the definition of the criteria for membership of particular religious groupings.

3. Christianity in the form of organized churches may be described as historically the most stable form of Christianity. "Church" here, however, should not be understood in the sense of a particular organizational type, since the social organization of Church Christianity has undergone characteristic changes in the course of history.

4. The churches' existing view of themselves, which in the Catholic Church, especially since the nineteenth century, has taken the form of ecclesiology, is "organization blind". This has two senses. First, the theory has no place for the real weaknesses of the organization, and, second, the organizational aspects of the Church appear in the theory only in the mediated concepts of "office", "hierarchy" or "papacy".

The last premise leads directly into our specific analysis. The specific feature of the Church as an organization (more especially in the Catholic Church than in the Protestant churches) is that, although it has experienced the general historical developments of functional differentiation, bureaucratization and socialization, in its own interpretation of itself it regards itself as endowed with a particular and essentially unchangeable structure of office. The Catholic Church in particular legitimates its identity not merely by the deposit of faith but also by particular elements of social structure. More precisely, the main elements of the organizational structure are defined as parts of the deposit of faith by an act of historical reconstruction (cf. I and II).

This means that existing problems of the *social form* of the Church are defined as theologically relevant so that they can be discussed within the Church only in religious terms, i.e., in terms of the "real" and the "identical", and not in terms of functional considerations.[6] This phenomenon can be seen repeatedly in the present discussions of the Joint Synod of the West German dioceses. Either any organizational change must start in the realm of what has been clearly defined in theology or (more especially) canon law, or quasi-theological legitimations must be constructed in order to obtain functionally necessary changes.

V

But this characteristic of religious organization is also an historical development and can perhaps be remedied by history.

For this purpose we must first inquire into the preconditions and causes of this sacralization of the organizational structures of the Church. Our thesis was that, in spite of the early introduction of administrative terms of Roman Law, the actual organization of the Church remained rudimentary throughout the Middle Ages, corresponding to the dominant segmentary, territorially based society. In this period there was no need for ecclesiology. The spiritual and the secular interpenetrated each other in the same way, whether a person was the subject of the pope or the emperor.

It was only with the gradual loss of Christianity's monopoly of interpreting reality that Western Christendom, for the first time since the Constantinian settlement, returned to a situation in which it was possible for it to see itself as a particular datum of society, separate from and quite often in opposition to the world. This change in the position of Christianity had two main causes, the split within Christianity itself and the emergence of competing interpretations of reality such as that of secular science.

The cultural and social processes of differentiation which have taken place since the Renaissance were factors which enabled

[6] For details see F.-X. Kaufmann, *Theologie in soziologischer Sicht* (Freiburg, 1973), pp. 127 ff., esp. 147 ff.

Christianity to see itself as Church, to define "Church" as the essence of Christianity, and contrast itself with the world. Following these processes of differentiation, however, the level of formal organization in the churches also rose considerably, with the result that the Church increasingly became a unique phenomenon, not just in its own interpretation of itself, but also in social life.

At this point a distinction must be made between the developments within Catholicism and those within Protestantism. In German-speaking countries at least, a greater use of the concept "Church" and an opposition between "Church" and "society" can be seen in Protestant as in Catholic theology since the nineteenth century,[7] although in Protestant theology the sacralization of the main organizational principles characteristic of Catholicism has been largely absent. For this reason our discussion applies mainly to the Catholic Church, which may also be regarded as the furthest development of the sociological type of the "Church". Significantly, it is also in the analysis of Protestant Christianity that the Church-sect dichotomy has proved inadequate.

In Catholicism, the tendency to sacralize the main organizational principles can be observed particularly clearly from the middle of the nineteenth century. Among its features are the growth of a specific cult of the pope since Pius IX, the development of a "triumphalist" ecclesiology in connection with the discussion of the schema on the Church at Vatican I and the subsequent definition of infallibility, regular wearing of the symbol of clerical office (the cassock) outside services, and the increased "veneration" of bishops and priests as representatives of the "holy".[8] It would take more detailed historical study to show how far this was the emergence of a new form of "Church re-

[7] On this, see esp. T. Rendtorff, *Kirche und Theologie* (Gütersloh, 1966), and J. Matthes, *Die Emigration der Kirche aus der Gesellschaft* (Hamburg, 1964).

[8] The thesis that the sacralization of organizational structures was a reaction by the Catholic Church to Christianity's loss of its monopoly of general social meaning was first put forward and established by Karl Gabriel in *Die Entwicklung der Organisations- und Führungsstruktur der katholischen Kirche in der Neuzeit in wissens- und organisationssoziologischer Perspektive*, unpublished thesis in the Sociology Faculty of the University of Bielefeld, 1973.

ligion" based on characteristics of the organization, because some similar attitudes can be found in earlier periods. In this case, however, there is definitely a change in motivation, since the reverence felt for an episcopal ruler is not identical with that felt for a bearer of the power of ordination.

There is much to support the view that this tendency to sacralize the structural elements of Church organization should be regarded, like the simultaneous renaissance of the thomistic view of natural law, primarily as an unconscious strategy on the part of the Church to maintain its absolute sacral power in society. It can be seen as the establishment of a sub-sensory world to replace the lost monopoly of interpretation of society as a whole. This would then explain the development of the Catholic sub-culture, in terms of which the actual development of Catholicism in the second half of the nineteenth and the first half of the twentieth centuries may be described. This was a particular form of reaction by the Catholic Church to the experience of secularization and increasing social differentiation and one which kept the identity of Catholicism stable for more than a century. There are more and more signs that this phase of history is coming to an end.[9]

VI

The Catholic view of the Church has hitherto been based on the assumption of a homogeneous social substratum in which the social processes of the transmission of the faith worked smoothly and the "plausibility structures" (P. L. Berger) of Catholicism were secure. As long as the Catholic sub-culture was intact, as long as Catholics gravitated to fellow Catholics in other than religious connections because of their denominational allegiance, the predominantly organizational character of the modern structures of the Church was not apparent to believers. The Church could still be regarded as the "holy mother" and not as a bureaucratic organization, and the pope as the "holy father" and not as the hierocratic leader of a multi-national organization. There

[9] Cf. F.-X. Kaufmann, op. cit.; idem, "Wissenssoziologische Überlegungen zu Renaissance und Niedergang des katholischen Naturrechtsdenkens im 19. and 20. Jahrhundert", in F. Böckle and E. W. Böckenförde (eds.), Naturrecht in der Kritik (Mainz, 1973), pp. 126-64.

are increasing signs of a change in the perception of the Church by Catholics which is making the previous ecclesiastical legitimation of its own organizational structure implausible. In this situation two things seem to be needed, first a developing ecclesiology which would find room in its theory for the historical and socially based character of the Church,[10] and, second, a more systematic investigation of the real organizational structures of the Church above and below the level of the parish. Investigations of this sort may be expected to reveal a considerable gap between the actual structures of decision-making and the canonical authorities.

At the same time there are considerable problems in the way of religious socialization (i.e., the transmission of religious meanings to the next generation). When the Church is felt as an "organization", it has no hope of focusing the identification which is an essential condition for the transmission of its values. It seems that religious motivations can only be transmitted within social relations of a "community" rather than a "society" type, but no "ideology of community" can in the long run conceal the "societal" character of the dominant social relations in the Church. This means that one of the main problems of Church organization in the future will be to encourage, and give ecclesiastical status to, social units of the group type, precisely because they conflict with the dominant principles of Church organization deriving from canon law. This is the legitimate core of the "spirit of anti-institutionalism" which, not least as a result of Karl Rahner's theology, seems to be a characteristic religious motivation of our time. It is not destruction, but growing complexity and diversity, of ecclesiastical organization, a deliberate mixing of formal and informal structural elements, which seems to offer the greatest hopes for the future of the Church as a religious organization.[11]

[10] This demand has also been made and defended by Leo Dullaart, "Kirche und Ekklesiologie. Die Institutionenlehre Arnold Gehlens als Frage an den Kirchenbegriff in der gegenwärtigen systematischen Theologie", unpublished dissertation in the University of Münster (Fachbereich Katholische Theologie), 1972. For the Protestant churches, cf. Yorick Spiegel, *Kirche als bürokratische Organisation* (Munich, 1969).

[11] On this, see esp. N. Luhmann, "Die Organisierbarkeit von Religionen

A development of this sort seems to be taking place already on the fringes of the Church. Student communities, action groups, meditation groups, family groups and similar very unstable groups sustain and develop broadly Christian religious motivations alongside and in opposition to the official Church organization. Their lack of ecclesiastical legitimacy seems to make a large contribution to their social instability. There is a simultaneous growth of the "ecclesiastical apparatus", at least where the churches have the financial resources for it. This apparatus does not become more Christian by cutting itself off from the tendencies to formalization, division of labour, the introduction of multidimensional hierarchy and control of effectiveness. These tendencies arise out of the historical situation of the Church in a highly differentiated society, and can only be rejected at the cost of social impotence. One of the criteria by which an ecclesiology should be judged is its ability to incorporate both these lines of development into its theory.

Translated by Francis McDonagh

---

und Kirchen", in J. Wössner (ed.), *Religion im Umbruch* (Stuttgart, 1972), pp. 245-85.

PART III
THE SOCIOLOGY OF ECCLESIASTICAL INSTITUTIONS

Jean Remy and Liliane Voyé

Informal Groups in the
Present-Day Church:
A Sociological Analysis

AT THE present time we are witnessing an important multiplication of what are called informal groups. These are known by various names, that of "community" occurring very frequently, but they all have a certain number of morphological characteristics in common. We are particularly concerned with small groups which arise in connection with very different questions and which, even if they are directed towards a form of activity external to themselves, find their dynamic basic in interpersonal relations.

The Church is no stranger to this tendency. In the Church, too, there are many such groups which for the most part bring together those Christians who are counted among the most active of its members. It is not the first time that this has happened in the history of the Church, but it would be fallacious to see only a simple repetition of the past in the movement that is taking place today. It is advisable to link the present tendency with the problems of an individualizing society that arouses in people both a desire to control their own destiny and a feeling of reserve towards large-scale organization.

Faced with the proliferation of these informal groups, we are bound to question their meaning, in particular within the Church, as well as the cause and the interest of these groups. That is the question we shall try to answer in the following pages.

To begin with, we would like to distinguish three distinct, though complementary, lines of inquiry.

I. THE PSYCHO-SOCIOLOGICAL LINE OF INTERPRETATION

Analysis along psycho-sociological lines is something we shall only develop very briefly. In fact, this approach is interesting in two ways. First, it allows other lines of inquiry—social and cultural—to emerge more clearly. Secondly, it puts us on our guard against a perspective marked by too psychological a bias, which would explain the way in which these informal groups are flourishing by taking into consideration only modern man's isolation, which on this interpretation would stimulate the multiplication of those groups within which man feels he can communicate, share and be appreciated for his own sake. Of course, as we shall show, such an explanation is not to be rejected, but it would be erroneous to see in it the exclusive cause of the multiplication of small groups.

Given these reservations, let us see how the context of urban life modifies the way in which the individual fits into social life and changes his capacity for interaction and expression. It can in fact be established that, at the psycho-sociological level, the urban context is characterized by moving from a simple to a complex system of proximity to other people. The simple system—such as is found within a family or in a village—gives rise to frequent personalized relationships between the members of the group who, in other respects, have only rare and limited relationships with the outside world. The complex system of interaction that is specific to the urban environment is, on the other hand, characterized by the multiplication of functional relationships (that is to say, those with a utilitarian aim). These are distinct from personal relationships (that is to say, those on an affective basis) and are separated from them by an entire scale of relationships of variable intensity and intimacy corresponding to the variety of the individual's links with other people.

It is in this kind of context that informal groups multiply, and its characteristics, which we have just briefly summarized, provide a convenient starting-point for asking about their significance. Do these groups help the individual to fit better and more quickly into the complex networks of relationships that are woven by the urban environment or are they, on the contrary, an indication of withdrawal and marginalization? Do they help to establish personal relationships within these networks or do they on the contrary form groupings shut in on themselves? According to whether it is the first or the second half of these two questions that is answered affirmatively, the meaning of these small groups is entirely different.

If they are seen as forming a springboard for fitting the individual into the complexity of the networks of communication and interaction to which the urban environment gives rise, then they form an effective area of apprenticeship for a life marked by risk and the absence of affective protection. If on the contrary they are experienced as withdrawal, entailing the minimum of necessary relationships that are needed for the individual to gain a certain equilibrium, then these groups could above all be sought out by those who, uncomfortable in the anonymity and functional quality of urban life, are looking for an affective security by limiting their contacts to those capable of bearing a personal character.

The two questions we have just put forward do not of course exhaust the considerations opened up by the psycho-sociological line of inquiry. Thus, instead of making the needs of the individual and of his relationships with other people our starting-point, as we have done, we could approach the problem by analysing the social usage of the word "community" as opposed to the social usage of the words "authority" and "fatherhood". Such an approach would mean our bringing out the fact that, in certain environments, the term "authority" possesses only negative connotations, while it is often in the same environments that the term "community" is surrounded by positive connotations—although these environments do not exclude but on the contrary encourage the emergence in their midst of informal leaders of a charismatic type who sometimes exercise an authority that is subject to relatively little control. One can, for example, consider the Auroville community in India which functions under the absolute and multivalent authority of its "mother". Nothing is done in any field without her approval; whether it is a question of economic production, of marriage, of the choice of a profession, etc., the conditions under which her leadership is exercised prevent any critical distancing or aloofness with regard to her. It is in fact a question of leadership founded on trust and personal knowledge, inducing a total surrender to the "mother" by all the members of this community.

It seems to us that this example shows clearly how sociological analysis enables one to be more objective and distant than the spontaneous reaction which would tend to understand the word "community" as covering a system of egalitarian relationships. Sociological analysis indeed emphasizes that, if community implies the existence of interpersonal relationships (which is what generally gives the word a positive connotation today), it is far from excluding the phenomenon of an authority which can be extremely powerful but which as such escapes one's immediate attention, which tends to give every form of authority a negative connotation.

II. The Cultural Line of Interpretation

In following the cultural line of interpretation, we shall analyse the forms of representation and the images by means of which society understands itself and from which individuals and particular groups define their projects. From this point of view, we shall now try to define a certain number of elements which together structure an interpretation of collective life, which in its turn provides a useful point of reference for each of these.

1. *The Birth of Small Groups in the Framework of valuing Autonomy and Spontaneity*

Contemporary man, stimulated by the discoveries of science and by the conditions of life offered him by the urban environment, seeks to control not only everything that surrounds him but also himself and claims a power of choice and of free expression in all fields. Several elements provide evidence of this deep-seated tendency.

(a) *Contrasts in time and space*

Earlier society made a contrast between the week and Sunday. During the week, society was dispersed and men lived in the fields and in the neighbourhoods; Sunday was a period of intense collective life, lived in the centre of the village or the town. Religious activity played a central role during this period of intensity. It was the privileged occasion for people meeting each other and gave birth to complementary activities (like the market) or competing ones (such as cafés) which came to reinforce the function of gathering together which it exercised and the life which it attracted to the centre of the village or the town.

Present-day society has changed the meaning of this contrast in time and space. In fact, it is during the week that people now tend to gather together in the urban centres to which they are called by their work and that collective life is at its most intense. On Sunday, on the other hand, social life is diluted. Sunday is the time of leisure, the privileged moment when everyone withdraws to his own home, sees his family and friends or leaves for the country. In this context, Sunday is generally an important moment for the building up of affective capital, but it is no longer a moment of intensity as far as collective life is concerned. It forms part of the leisure activity that extends over each weekend, is frequently taken up each evening, and reaches its peak at holiday time, but it is only rarely any longer the moment when important matters are settled and the collectivity reaffirms its identity.

The significance of Sunday for collective life has been reduced, and the same applies to town and village centres. Projective tests are very enlightening on this subject. If in a sociological survey, a person is asked to design the town in which he or she would like to live, the focal point of his or her design is very often the choice of where he or she wants to live. This thus appears as the psychological centre that provides the starting-point from which all the remainder is seen and around which everything else is placed later.

This reversal in the significance of privileged periods and spaces allows us to understand a change in the significance of religion. Formerly it was a means of collective expression, but today it tends to become a privileged area of expression for individual life. Indeed, the increased value that is placed upon leisure time and the central role played by where one lives are in our society accompanied by an establishment of the individual as the focus of choice and the criterion for judgment. Without any doubt, such a tendency is encouraged by the media which more and more submit to the judgment and appreciation of their readers, listeners or viewers a spectrum of opinion and points of view among which each individual has the opportunity of choosing on the supposition of a certain, though very relative, knowledge of the case.

(b) *The contrast of private and public*

To this contrast in time and space we must add another contrast, that between the private and the public spheres. This is just as much a characteristic of time and space as of activities.

If one breaks down the elements that make up the concept of "private", one establishes that it designates an area within which the person or group concerned has the possibility and the capability of controlling what is happening without having to submit to the consideration or the intervention of an external power. A schematic description of the content can be provided by saying that it deals with extra-professional life and in particular of leisure life—over which authority renounces all power to the extent that it regards this area as lacking social motivity. The contrast between private and public, which can be defined by using the contrary characteristics of the pair as a starting-point, tends to a certain extent to replace the contrast between sacred and profane. The category of sacred, like that of public, refers to matters that are important for collective life, while the category of profane, like that of private, refers to matters lacking collective significance. The overlapping of these two opposing pairs is nevertheless ambiguous. Indeed, while formerly it was the Church's public character and its great visibility in the centre of the town or village, at the side of other official buildings, that expressed its sacred character, today the value that is placed on it is increasingly withdrawn from its involvement in the areas of daily life which are ultimately assigned to various activities other than cultural ones—whether it is a question of housing or of a cultural centre.

In this way one can state that, from now on, numerous religious activities take their place in the framework of extra-professional life—that is to say that part of life regarded as not important by a society dominated by economic considerations—and that these increasingly belong to private life which, although any absolute and unique authority is avoided, is controlled by individuals and the small groups that they form.

(c) *The contrast between the ideologically neutral and the ideologically weighted*

Yet a third contrast arises to structure the perceptions by which everyone today tends to find his bearings. What is involved is the contrast between what is perceived as ideologically neutral and what is perceived as having ideological characteristics. One example serves to illuminate this thesis. The idea that education should be obligatory up to the age of fifteen or sixteen and that the period of schooling should not be left to the judgment of the father of the family, still less to that of the children, is a rule that in our countries is generally seen as a matter of course and as lacking any ideological implication. Of course, what is involved is a restraint upon people's freedom, but it is understood as being promotional and not repressive. The rule must therefore be imposed on all, in an unquestionable manner. On the other hand, belonging to a political party or to a church, as well as taking part in all the activities and lesser groupings that these organize, through the phenomenon of a kind of capillary attraction, are regarded as having an ideological content. These are therefore left to everyone's free choice, without any pressure being exercised.

This contrast has a very deep effect on social life, throughout its various activities as well as throughout the periods and places where these take place. In this field, the case of Belgium is particularly enlightening. During the last century and at the beginning of this, a double infrastructure developed based on the one hand on the Socialist Party and on the other on the Catholic Church. These two institutions competed to establish professional associations, leisure organizations, retail co-operatives, building societies, etc., and whether one used one or the other of this range of services was determined by one's ideological commitment. It was on a basis of identity or opposition between the ideological content of these services and the places they occupied and that of those using them that a relationship of trust or mistrust was defined. After a certain number of years, less value came to be placed on the ideological content of these services and places,

and most of the time it is services and places that are perceived
as ideologically neutral that are preferred by most users, whatever their own ideology may be. This without a doubt explains
the decline of "parish circles" and "people's centres" to the bene-
fit of "cultural centres" and again the near-disappearance of
retail co-operatives—socialist or Catholic—which find themselves
edged out by the large stores or supermarkets which—thanks to
what is in effect a disguising of their true nature—are seen as
ideologically neutral.

On the basis of this example, one can grasp that what is perceived as ideologically neutral is in fact that which offers the
least explanation of itself and which as a result tends to be the
most constraining. In fact, the category of things with an ideological content supposes the existence of differing opinions
and demands a choice. Thus, on the question of abortion, everyone claims to have an opinion and a point of view. In contrast,
in areas which are perceived as ideologically neutral, there is a
compelling restraint, precisely because no divergence of opinion
with regard to them seems to be possible. This is the case with
regard to styles of clothing which everyone generally tends to
follow more or less without questioning them.

In the preceding pages we have tried to show three types of
important changes in the perceptions that structure the cultural
framework. In the first place, we have emphasized how the week
that has come to be the intense period of collective life when
people gather together, essentially around professional activities. In this context Sunday, associated with extra-professional
life and with the building up of affective capital, has lost its
collective importance and brought in its train dispersion and the
high value placed on the individual home. Secondly, we insisted
on the emergence, in the field of what is private, of activities,
places and periods that had little collective motivity, thus allowing
the expression of individual control and of spontaneity. Finally,
we concluded by emphasizing the decline, in a certain number
of fields, of what has an ideological content and the preference
granted to activities and places perceived as ideologically neutral.
By means of this analysis we have tried to show the importance

of the way in which perceptions are culturally structured, a structuring which determines the diffusion of shared categories and thus modifies the significance of various phenomena.

This applies among other things to religious phenomena. Once perceptions have been changed and these new perceptions have spread to give rise to new shared categories, religious phenomena undergo a profound change of meaning without any change taking place in their formal content. Let us return to the three contrasts that we have analysed and try to measure their effect on the religious phenomenon.

Sunday, we have seen, is now associated with extra-professional life, with the breaking up of collective life, with the home, with the building up of affective capital. But it remains a moment of intensity for the religious life, just as it was when Sunday was at the same time a moment of intensity for collective life. This change that has taken place in the way in which Sunday is perceived tends to have repercussions on the content of the religious life that occurs then. Like Sunday, it tends to be fitted into the framework of extra-professional life and of cultural activities.

We then saw that the area described as public was concerned with activities considered as having a high degree of social motivity, which implied control by some authority. In a society dominated by economic considerations, the field of religion loses its social motivity and control is relaxed with regard to it. It depends more and more on the private life of individuals and thus on their personal choice.

Finally, to the extent that the religious sphere is perceived as having an ideological content, that is to say, as not imposing itself in the manner of an objective reality but, on the contrary, as supposing a choice, an option, and to the extent that moreover, as we have just seen, it increasingly forms part of the private sphere it becomes uncomfortable for it to intervene with the public authorities on the basis of an equal footing of power.

These various elements with regard to the change in meaning of the religious sphere that insist on its forming part of the cultural framework lead very naturally to a higher value being placed on forms of social relationships centred on the small group, whose initiative springs from the grass-roots and which shows itself to be hesitant vis-à-vis an organization exterior to itself. One is thus able to gauge here the entire effect of a new structuring of collective perceptions for the meaning of the religious sphere, independently of any change of the formal content of this.

2. *The Small Group's Links with the Outside World*

Once small groups of this kind have been formed, one can ask how these see their links with the outside world. This is the question we shall focus on for the moment.

Certain members of the small group can draw their inspiration from a vision of harmony and integration with regard to society as a whole. In this case, they will gladly see a link between what is experienced within the small group and what ought to be valid for society at large. What is thus seen in the small group is a relationship of harmony with strong affective implications. Moreover, those who align themselves according to this perspective will have a tendency to think that society at large would be profoundly changed if everyone were able to think and live according to the same methods and styles as those who govern the functioning of the small group. Intense interpersonal relationships are consequently regarded as being that which will bring about a profound modification of the world, and the supreme witness borne by the Christian is thought to be that which he can give through the quality of the interpersonal relationships he enjoys with others.

In contrast with this, other members of the small group think of their link with society as a whole in terms of conflict. The experience that is valid for the microcosmic group cannot be transposed to society as a whole, which needs other modes of intervention if it is to be changed. In this context the small communities set up as their function to try to build up a web of relationships that are sufficiently autonomous to give rise to a counter-culture, particularly by offering an escape-route for a family caught up in the web of ordinary social relationships. This in fact implies entering into an anticipatory system which supposes the acceptance of forms institutionalized by the dominant form of society and notably of the system of remuneration this uses. Thus, instead of simply giving an interpersonal dimension to the culture that is already established, what one wants to do by means of the autonomy of the grass-roots community is to create possibilities for a counter-culture. The grass-roots community conceived in this way can for some people be a group of withdrawal: a "warm" community which allows one to withdraw from a world that is regarded as aggressive and disordered. This type of reaction is common for those social classes subjected to intense social insecurity.

III. The Social Line of Interpretation

The essence of a culture is to furnish different social groups with the categories through which they can communicate and interpret their experience. Nevertheless, this common language finds itself appropriated in different ways by different social groups which each give it a specific connotation. It is thus convenient in this analysis to take account of the elements of the social structure and to follow a social line of interpretation that can be defined as referring to the networks of interaction on the basis of which power is organized, shared or stabilized.

In following this line for the analysis of small groups, one is led to state that similar groups can have opposite effects according to whether they arise within this or that social environment. In this way a group based on interpersonal relationships that places a high value on the Christian as universal brother can have a very different meaning according to the environment from which it draws its membership. For a bourgeois and intellectual environment, it is perhaps a way of disguising social oppositions that have become intolerable by transcending them without making any real change in the situation. This function would furthermore be better accomplished if a minority within these groups were drawn from within another social milieu. In this way, the majority would have the happy feeling of encountering people from every social class and background. Following this line, one can ask to what extent one is not observing, within the Church after the Council, the seizure of power by certain groups—intellectuals and certain types of militant, for example. From a sociological point of view, one could ask oneself what the consequences would be for a church which had to function as if it were composed essentially either of intellectuals or of militants, these latter rarely exceeding ten per cent of the total population, whatever may be the field in which one envisages them taking part.

Certainly we could linger over drawing out the meaning that informal groups thus take on in the different social groups within which they are formed. However, we prefer to consider two questions more particularly. First, we shall ask ourselves what the meaning is that such groups have for the middle class. Secondly, we shall analyse the problem of informal groups within the framework of social movements. We shall see here that similar groups, operating perhaps within the same cultural categories, take on different meanings according to the environment which gives rise to them.

1. Informal Groups and the Middle Class

We shall consider the middle class not as a group to which people simply belong and which can be characterized by the intersection of relatively objective criteria, such as the level of income, the level of education, etc., but rather as a reference group that aims at a social life-style and presupposes cultural isolation and insecurity. In fact, people who find themselves in this kind of situation could be defined negatively in two ways. They no longer belong to the environment and the culture of the working class, which they reject, and they do not yet belong to the upper classes which they try to judge themselves by without yet being capable, as these latter are, of endowing their possessions and their behaviour with the characteristics of prestige.

The example of choosing where to go on holiday is enlightening on this subject. People of the middle class will normally want to go on holiday to certain places which have been endowed with prestige by the upper classes of the population. There they encounter the cultural consumption of goods which have been endowed with prestige by others and the prestige of which one tries to share by the very fact of consumption. In this way they enter on a process of continual outbidding, since, as soon as middle-class people try in this way to appropriate the goods that up till then the upper classes have been keeping for themselves, the upper classes create new indicators of differentiation which summon up a new desire to imitate on the part of the middle class.

Often the same thing happens with regard to social relationships. Middle-class people lose or reject the relationships characteristic of working-class surroundings, based on mutual aid within the context of spatial proximity, but do not yet enjoy the networks of relationships that are not based on locality and that are specific to the upper classes. Made insecure in this way by the fact of these two negative definitions, middle-class people will, in certain cases, find in the interpersonal groups that arise, notably in the Church, a privileged area where they are able to flourish. It is not only that these groups will help them to endow themselves with a certain wealth of relationships, but again they encourage the transformation of their relationship with culture. The middle class thus in general constitutes a public that is specifically motivated to take part in small informal groups, to the extent that these appear as effective means of interiorization of the rules of the dominant culture.

2. Informal Groups and the Social Movement

Defining the social movement as a movement capable of transforming social priorities without having for this purpose to be mediated by an organization, we shall now ask ourselves what meaning informal groups can have in this framework.

In its first stage, the social movement—just like the middle class—finds itself confronted by a problem of cultural insecurity, but this is of an entirely different type. Indeed what is involved for this movement is to spread among a whole series of people pride in not being made to feel guilty or to blame according to the norms of the dominant groups. This does not occur without giving rise to a deep sense of insecurity which is able to evaporate in groups with intense affective implications. This was the case during the last century for the working-class movement which developed, often in cafés, meeting-places that ended by forming working-class "communities" with a combative aim, where the family as such was frequently called into question, a little in the way in which it is in certain communities at the present day.

In the second stage of its evolution, the problem arises in different terms for the social movement. It is no longer henceforth so much a question of creating this pride of belonging presented as something pre-existing but rather of spreading a counter-feeling of guilt throughout the whole of society by trying to give it an uneasy conscience by reference to generally accepted norms. Here too small groups will often play a central role in this process of diffusion, but although they can present the same type of external morphology as in the first stage they have a totally different social meaning.

IV. CONCLUSION

An explanation that aims to be comprehensive cannot ignore any of these three lines of analysis but must work out various ways in which these can be combined. One thus avoids the trap of a unilateral explanation of informal groups. These must therefore be re-situated within a multi-dimensional space if one wants to evaluate their meanings and their consequences as justly as possible. It would also seem to us a very reductionist explanation to attribute the reasons and the meaning of the spontaneous development of these small groups exclusively to a feeling of isolation in large conurbations and a feeling of the insufficiency of the nuclear family, regarded as too poor in pluriform relationships, in a context which allows creation an increased field of autonomy.

Taking these various lines of analysis into consideration has allowed us to grasp the diversity of the demands that are made on small groups and in particular on those based on the religious life.

We may consequently ask to what extent, alongside a Church regarded by some people as supplying various services in a client relationship, there is not developing a plurality of forms of membership through informal groups with different meanings, without in other respects certain more collective forms of encounter and liturgy being excluded. Whatever the case may be, one can, without risk of error, note the present flourishing, within the Church as elsewhere, of informal groups insisting on the quality of personal relationships and showing hesitation with regard to organization.

Let us nevertheless note that this distancing from the organization is not to be confused with the rejection of an organization of services for which the necessity of an infrastructure is not involved. All the same, it is possible that it may be a typical fact of Western Christianity and specifically of Catholicism to associate closely the stability of the institution with its organizational development and with the desire to integrate. The question then arises of knowing to what extent these groups need to be integrated and for what purpose it would be suitable to integrate them. From the heuristic point of view, it would be an interesting problem to ask those who want to integrate how they would justify this desire. They seem, indeed, in this way to be going against patterns which tend today to structure our daily reactions in a dominant manner, both in the religious life and in most of the other spheres of social life.

Translated by Robert Nowell

Peter Rudge

The Sociology of Conflict and Ecclesiastical Life

THE tension between sociology and religion is evident in the attitudes to conflict: there are differences in value systems between a scientific sociology and a personal and emotive religion.

I

Conflict, to the student of social behaviour, is a phenomenon to be observed and analysed; it is objectified as a thing that can be considered in its own right and about which predictions can be made.

On the other hand, to the religionist, conflict appears to be foreign to the ethos of the Christian life. A ready response is that dissidence is contrary to our Lord's teaching, that it has no place in the life of the Church. Witness the dominical precept to love one's neighbour; the exhortation to be of one mind; the fruits of the spirit is love, joy, peace, long-suffering, gentleness, meekness, and so on; the Pauline horror at divisions in the Church at Corinth.

Of course, this reaction is superficial, as any biblical scholar would testify. There are, for instance, our Lord's words that he came not to bring peace but a sword, that a person's enemies would be those of his own household. St Paul used the imagery of warfare, for example, in Ephesians 6. 10–20, and, in dealing with dissension in the Church, said, "there must be factions among you in order that those who are genuine among you may be recognized" (1 Cor. 11. 19).

Nevertheless, the impression may remain that there is no room for contention in the Church, that the value system to which the Church subscribes involves a rejection of conflict. The rejection may seem to a sociologist to be a weakness of religion in comparison with which the scientific attitude is enlightened. But it is only fair to point out that the attitude to conflict that is found in religion is not confined to that area of life alone but is common to many other fields of human endeavour. Musicians can be equally intolerant of discords as being foreign to the value systems of the musical world although some modern composers set themselves the task of creating harmony by the constructive use of discords. Likewise, a traditional and classical artist looks only on goodness, truth and beauty; whereas in modern art one often finds an attempt to use clashes of colour and form as the raw material of a new concept of beauty and meaning.

Moreover, the Church as an institution shares with other organizations certain patterns of leadership,[1] very few of which show any leniency towards conflict. Taking the Weberian categories in turn, the traditional forms of leadership developed mainly in an era of comparative stability—the maintenance of the *status quo* was the objective. Traditional organization in society or in the Church is highly resistant to change. Tradition mutes the dissenting voice and the weight of ancient authority and the wisdom of the elders leaves little room for the innovator or rebel.

Charismatic authority, while thriving on hostility towards an external enemy, likewise has little tolerance of internal chal-

[1] For a study of styles of leadership in Churches see Peter F. Rudge, *Ministry and Management* (London, 1968; French trans., Paris, 1971); also "Styles of Administration in Churches in their Theological Presuppositions", *Social Sciences and the Churches*, ed. C. L. Mitton (Edinburgh, 1972). There is the beginning of a study of conflict in *Ministry and Management*, 35-36 (55-56 in the French edition).

For a sociological study of conflict see Lewis A. Coser, *The Functions of Social Conflict* (London, 1968). Coser provides a technical vocabulary and a series of propositions on the positive value of conflict in many spheres of life, including ecclesiastical organizations. His introductory chapter traces the history of the sociological study of conflict which indicates a reticence on the part of sociologists to consider it constructively. Coser's study marks a significant attempt to develop a positive analysis.

lenges to it. Such leaders can wield so much dominion over their disciples that the ranks are closed, the dissenters purged, the rebels excluded.

Even within the bureaucratic pattern of leadership is there little room for variance. That pattern of organization which is based on rationality and is seemingly akin to the very ethos of scientific sociology itself is notorious for its harshness in dealing with conflict. This is not only so when the Church assumes a bureaucratic form of authority but in the ruthless world of commercial life as well.

The charge of adopting an inadequate attitude to conflict cannot be laid solely at the doors of religion—it is common to many walks of life.

II

Such an attitude is not thereby excused but it is possible to see —in the rejection of conflict as being contrary to one's value system or as a threat to one's leadership—that there is the possibility of a more scientific attitude. Conflict can be considered more dispassionately if it is external. Even though there may be little intellectual refinement, there is certain native intelligence about outside hostility. The externalization of opposition can be a powerful internal force to serve the ends that a leader has in mind. An external enemy is a useful thing, a statement which goes a long way towards objectifying conflict as a thing to be . studied and, for the shrewd leader, to be manipulated.

Opponents of a reorganization in the Church of England, a strongly traditional body, found it easy to rally support for rejecting the Ridley Report of 1956 by playing on people's fears, by using emotive words such as "streamlining", "rationalizing", "bureaucratizing" and "Americanizing". The establishment was being threatened, there was a common enemy, and so the ranks were closed and the thrust was blunted. People perceived the proposals of the Paul Report to replace the freehold of the clergy with a leasehold as a threat to established order. The threat was seen as coming from outside and the instinctive response was to reject the proposals.

As with established Churches, so with sects. An external enemy is a strong unifying force. An outside challenge, either real or imagined, binds people together in withstanding it. The Jehovah's Witnesses preach impending doom, the Seventh Day Adventists the immediate return of our Lord; the Exclusive Brethren are made more exclusive by the openness of the Open Brethren. Charismatic leaders thrive on conflict with forces in the world; and it is a well-known device to distract people from internal problems by drawing attention to an outside threat.

To a bureaucratic type of leader, conflict is externalized by invoking the sacredness of order over against chaos—conflict is a threat to established ways. Smother innovation with red tape, exclude the dissident by sheer weight of numbers, show up the rebels as those who would overthrow the system. Sometimes the Roman Catholic Church is referred to as being monolithic, intolerant of opposition, disorder and conflict. Most religious orders have taken time to be accepted, Gallicanism has always been a contentious issue and the recent developments in the Dutch Church have been looked upon with some alarm.

Yes, conflict is a thing—something to be excluded, to be externalized. To do so is an intuitive reaction for self-protection, the preservation of the tradition or the charism or the system. As long as it is external, it is safe—until breaking-point is reached, in the form of revolution.

III

To internalize conflict is a difficult and dangerous operation. The Church has always allowed some internal conflict for there has been a conciliar element in it, the councils being one way of allowing diversity of views or keeping them within acceptable proportions. In the same way, the Westminster form of parliamentary democracy has a role for Her Majesty's Loyal Opposition, the legal system has provision for a case to be defended as well as prosecuted and the process of canonization allows a place for the devil's advocate.

The Council of Acts 15 was an attempt to regulate internal conflict in the early Church. The great definitive councils of the fourth and fifth centuries sought to resolve the divergent opinions within the Church although the doors were soon shut against people like Origen. The councils of the fifteenth century had a tenuous existence. It became much easier to cope with an external enemy in the form of Protestantism in the sixteenth century and the subsequent councils were not so much an indication of tolerance but a means of excluding it as in the case of the Council of Trent or the First Vatican Council. The Second Vatican Council lowered the threshold of tolerance—under Pope John XXIII, conflict was internalized. The problem since his death has been to determine what level of conflict is appropriate, if it can be accepted at all.

If the conciliar movement indicate macro-dimension of internal conflict, the techniques of the behavioural school such as group dynamics have been the micro-expression of the same thing. The development has meant a lowering of the threshold of conflict—groups have been opened to tensions and expression has been allowed to diversify. The face-to-face group is a place where conflict can be fully internalized, recognized and accepted —so it is hoped. The somewhat sad history of the group dynamics movement is that the hope has not always been realized. Conflicts too great to be contained have destroyed groups and people have been deeply hurt and offended. Another form of division has been created—between the "labbed" and the "unlabbed", the "enlightened" and the "mass of common people". In parishes, cleavages have developed between those in the know and those to whom the technique is just another gimmick.

At levels between universal councils and small groups, there have been the same difficulties in coping with internal conflict. Illustrations can be found in religious orders, most of which in origin have been innovating bodies, expressing a new charism, fresh insights, a renewed sense of vocation, often in opposition to the established Church. But because of their loyalty to the Church they have proved to be a useful mechanism for internalizing conflict. However, many orders have taken on characteristics of the establishment—their history, their traditions, their apostolates, their property have led to a settled pattern of life. There have, however, been those within the orders who have felt the winds of change, who have opened their windows to the world after the example of Pope John, who have sought to be true to the spirit of the Second Vatican Council. There has been incipient conflict within the orders but often no means by which to control it. Some congregations have almost fallen apart; others have been through traumas of internal revolution. There have been changes in rule, in the daily office, in dress, in the content of their journals—and only wise leadership and the realization of new challenges from the world have enabled the period of conflict to be safely negotiated. In one way, part of the answer lay in establishing a recognizable system of internal communication to supersede an earlier organ which provided an open forum for a great diversity of views, especially of a vocal minority.

Conflict, then, is neither a wholly bad thing to be shunned and excluded, nor a wholly good thing to be welcomed and given free rein. The problem is to determine the optimum level of conflict and to provide mechanisms for its expression and control.

IV

In cybernetic terms, conflict is an indication of variety. How does one deal with variety? A simple and easy solution is to kill it but then one has lost the benefits that variety can bring. Allowing too much variety, on the other hand, can lead to confusion and chaos. The answer lies in matching the variety in the world by creating in the control mechanism a capacity to cope with it. If you are faced with a skilful football team, for instance, one way to deal with it is to kill off all the opposing players—that would kill the variety in their attack but it would also stop the game. To march one's own team off the field so that the opponents could knock in goals at will would not be much fun for them. The quality of the game depends on the matching variety in the two teams and victory comes from having just that margin of variety greater than the opponents.

Treat conflict in the same way. Accept the conflict, welcome what it is that prompts the opposing views or actions and create a new synthesis out of all the varied elements. This is easier said than done, but it is the real test of leadership—not least leadership in the Churches at the local level and all levels to the universal. It is all the more difficult in the life of the Church because of the inherent prejudice against conflict and the defensive desire to exclude it. But it is all the more necessary because of the vocation of the Church, with its ministry of reconciliation. In Christ there is neither Jew nor Greek, male nor female, bond nor free—but none of these elements can be by-passed nor their significance ignored. How can they be included unless tensions are brought out into the open, faced and then resolved?

All this presupposes a structure for the management of conflict. The point of providing structures is not just to contain diversity within the organization in order that, in the Churches' case, it can fulfil its all-embracing and reconciling work. The virtue of structuring conflict is also to make it external to the person, though remaining internal to the Church. If there is an opportunity for expressing views, these opinions can stand on their own in an objective way, able to be recognized, considered and examined. The absence of a structure within which to express one's feelings means that antagonisms are left in the personal realm either to disturb a person and fester within him or to break out in untoward and uncharitable ways. Against the latter, there are biblical injunctions—this sort of contention is contrary to the Christian ethos. But structured and managed diversity is not foreign to the Christian ethic—this is what the sociology of conflict has been witnessing to. What has been missing is the provision of an adequate structure for conflict—more than that, what has been missing is a theological rationale for such structures in the Church.

What that theology, that structure, is can be stated very simply. There is a clear correlation between the strong and fundamental emphasis on organic imagery in the New Testament and the view of management expressed in organic or systemic terms. The test in this case is the validity of this theology of structure for the management of conflict.

Certainly there is room for diversity within the body as St Paul points out in 1 Corinthians 12—the members always have the opportunity for independent action but the real harmony lies in their interdependent relationship within the body as a whole. Likewise, in Ephesians 4, the process of growth and maturing into the fullness of Christ necessarily involves the overcoming of tensions and the recognition of the dignity of the gifts that the members have.

In its organizational expression, the emphasis is upon flexibility rather than the rigidity of departments or sections, upon a deliberate introduction of factors and influences from the outside world, upon the continual adjustment and readjustment of the structures to meet new needs, upon the role of the leader as a negotiator of a new consensus and as the monitor of subsequent action.

V

So far, so good. But there still may be conflicts in organizational life of the kind that are contrary to the Christian ethic. It is easy to treat these as personal misdemeanours and blame them on the corruption of human nature. That may be the cause, but it is also worth considering them as diagnostic indicators. What is manifest as conflict at a personal level may in fact reflect a structural disorder. The resentment of a curate against his vicar or a clerk against his senior diocesan executive may not be primarily due to the perversity of either or both but to the inadequacy of the career structure. The absence of a career structure could produce frustration which is given vent in the form of uncharitableness. New provision for career development can remove the cause of the difficulty and give rise to new co-operation between the two in place of the former antagonism.

There can be hurt feelings and animosity between a parson and his bishop, a parishioner and his parish priest, a religious and his superior. Such feelings may not be so much a matter of personal intractability but an indication of structural deficiency. Perhaps there has not been an adequate forum for the expression of views on a particular matter or the agenda may not have been constructed with sufficient care or the senior person may have confused his role as president or chairman of a legislative body with that as superior in an executive structure. This commonly occurs where a bishop is president of a synod, a vicar is chairman of a parish council or a religious superior is chairman of a chapter.

Resentment can build up in a superior officer over the slackness or failure in performance by a subordinate, but the fault may be in the structure of the superior-subordinate relationship—the job description which should include the specific details of a person's responsibility may not have made the lines of responsibility clear.

The abhorrence of conflict in the Church on the grounds of the Christian ethic or the externalization of it to engender a narrow and exclusive unity will not do. The objectifying of conflict as a thing which can be dealt with in a constructive way is the contribution of the sociology of conflict to ecclesiastical life. The management of conflict needs to be structured in such a way as to give it a full place within the Church, especially in this age of change—in an objective way so as to avoid any personal implications that would otherwise offend against Christian precepts. At the same time, the structure needs to be matched by the spiritual maturity of Christian leaders and people which rises above personal interests and animosities and leads to a genuine respect for the other person and his views.

Donald Warwick

The Centralization of Ecclesiastical Authority: An Organizational Perspective

FOR THE student of organizations one of the most striking features of the Roman Catholic Church is the high degree of centralization of authority in the papacy. Why did a Church which began as a loose assemblage of quasi-autonomous communities become a massive bureaucratic organization with power and authority concentrated in the pope? This paper presents an approach, based on recent work in the sociology of organizations, which may shed light on the processes of bureaucratization and papalization in the Church. The basic argument is that the present structure of authority is in large part a cumulative organizational response to a shifting and often threatening environment.

I. AN APPROACH TO ORGANIZATIONS

An organization is a set of explicitly co-ordinated and interdependent activities designed to achieve certain goals. While the Church and the U.S. Department of State differ in their goals and structures, both qualify as organizations because of their deliberate harnessing of human activity to collective ends. In this discussion, an organization will be viewed as an open system in constant interaction with its environment. The critical point is that the kinds of interactions which take place exert a direct influence on the internal structure of authority and decision-making. Some patterns are much more likely than others to stimulate hierarchy and centralization.

An organization's environment has both remote and proximate

elements. The remote environment consists of those socio-cultural, ecological and technological conditions with indirect effects on internal processes and structures. Among these are cultural —norms, patterns of social stratification and power blocs in international relations. In matters ranging from liturgy to styles of decision-making the Church has always been influenced by its remote environment. Our present concern, however, is primarily with the proximate environment. This has two interlocking subparts: the power setting and the operating environment.

The *power setting* consists of those actors who exert or can exert an immediate influence on the organization. Among these are controllers, those who have authority over the organization; clients; suppliers; allies; and adversaries, whether rivals or enemies.[1] Historically the most important controllers in the power setting of the Church have been temporal rulers, such as Constantine, who might also be political allies as well as clients. Adversaries, especially heretics and hostile rulers, also play a prominent role in the drama of papalization.

An organization's *operating environment* is the set of conditions in which it carries out its day-to-day work. Four such conditions are especially important: (1) complexity, or the number of elements comprising the environment and the intricacy of their connections; (2) uncertainty, or the degree of unpredictability; (3) threat, the extent to which the environment is perceived to be a source of losses or harm; and (4) dispersion, the geographic scope of an organization's activities and structures.

Church historians have been quite aware, in general terms, of the interdependence of the Church and the surrounding society. Most often, however, the conceptual models used to deal with this interaction have emphasized assimilation, imitation and, at the outer limit, integration. Without denigrating the importance of the assimilationist view, this paper will lay primary emphasis on the role of conflict, tension and compensatory moves in transactions with the environment. The gradual tightening of central authority will be viewed less as an imitation of societal patterns (a factor which cannot be discounted) than as a series of defensive responses aimed at dealing with uncertainty and threat.

[1] Cf. A. Downs, *Inside Bureaucracy* (Boston, 1967).

This paper advances four broad hypotheses about the role of Church-environment interactions in the centralization of the papacy. First, the growing complexity and dispersion of the Church in the early centuries created demands for a separate administrative hierarchy and formal mechanisms of co-ordinaion. Second, uncertainty and threats in the environment of the Church were often met by centralization and bureaucratization. Third, at critical points in Western history uncertainty and threat to the population at large generated pressures for a strong, active papacy to maintain or restore order. In other words, both threats to the Church itself and to the surrounding society had the same organizational effect. Fourth, strong demands for centralization also arose from the Church's controllers and political allies, most notably the Emperor Constantine. The following discussion, which is necessarily highly condensed, briefly examines Church history in the light of these hypotheses.

II. THE PRE-CONSTANTINIAN PERIOD (1–311)

In the primitive Church, little emphasis was placed on hierarchy, authority and orthodoxy. There was no papacy and no central bureaucracy. "In the pre-Nicene centuries the local *ekklesia* was largely self-sufficient and to a surprising degree autonomous. Unity among churches manifested itself in agreement on faith rather than in institutional structures. In fact, no permanent organizational machinery existed above the level of the local church."[2] Leadership was exercised by the bishop and, with him, the presbyters, but authority was also shared with the community.

The collegial model worked well as long as the communities remained small and geographically united. As the Church grew in size and covered a wider area, dispersion produced mounting problems of co-ordination. At the beginning the presbyters had worked on a close consultative basis with their bishops. As they scattered throughout the first missionary territories, it became

[2] J. E. Lynch, "Co-responsibility in the first five centuries: presbyteral colleges and the election of bishops", paper presented at the Symposium on Co-responsibility in the Church, sponsored by the Canon Law Society of America, 1972, p. 2.

very difficult to maintain this relationship. Gradually they began to function as heads of relatively independent communities, acting as deputies of the bishops. In a classic example of hierarchical differentiation, the bishops increasingly moved from pastoral to administrative roles. "The bishop instead of shaping policy for the local church with the advice of the presbyterate now served to transmit the policy set at a higher ecclesiastical level."[3]

Early environmental threats added to the pressure for line authority. These came in the form of schisms and heresies striking at the doctrinal foundations of Christianity. The first schisms grew out of the various Judaizing movements, such as the Ebionites. In the second and third centuries an even more serious challenge was presented by Gnosticism, a doctrine emphasizing, *inter alia*, the liberation of the soul from the prison of matter through *gnosis* or knowledge. Though its teachings are difficult to summarize, this syncretistic movement had great appeal because of its promise of salvation. For the early Christians, the challenge was immediate and non-academic—members were being lost.

The most enduring impact of the early heresies was their stimulation of organizational centralization. Although the Church was not well organized in the second century, the response to the challenges was amazingly similar in different areas. The common element in the various anti-heretical instruments was an emphasis on apostolic succession and doctrinal uniformity. "Soon the impact of the heresies led Christians to join the ideas of apostolic succession and of monarchical episcopacy, and thus began the emphasis on the uninterrupted chain of bishops who unite the present Church with apostolic times."[4] The heightened attention to the role of the bishop led to a further separation between himself and the presbyters. A second device to combat heresy was the definition of the canon of the New Testament. This measure served to undercut the claims of heretics to legitimation by apostolic teaching. The widely shared desire for doctrinal uniformity further gave rise to catechetical questions and answers which eventually became the Apostles' Creed. The

[3] *Ibid.*, p. 23.
[4] J. L. Gonzalez, *A History of Christian Thought, Vol. I, From the Beginnings of the Council of Chalcedon* (Nashville and New York, 1970), p. 150.

specific content of this affirmation of faith had a decided anti-heretical orientation. Finally, the uncertainty and threat created by the heresies set the stage for the emergence of theology. Without question the major impetus behind the first attempts at the systematic formulation of doctrine was the desire to promote the purity of the faith. The principal work of Irenaeus, for example, is titled *Adversus Haereses*, and is mainly a refutation of Gnosticism. The advent of theology contributed directly to centralization of authority through the unification of doctrine and indirectly by generating demands for authorities to monitor the increasing volume of sensitive publications.

III. CONSTANTINE TO THE REFORMATION

The conversion of Constantine in 312 led to an organizational merger with incalculable effects on the future of the Church. Bolstered by imperial favour, the Church took full advantage of its power position to win new converts to the faith. The resulting expansion of the catechumenate led to a rapid growth in the sheer size of the organization, greater geographic dispersion and a more complex operating environment. These developments created unprecedented problems of co-ordination, and paved the way to an expanded bureaucracy.

Constantine, for his part, also had an interest in a unified and well-organized Church. An experienced political leader, he saw in the Church a highly effective means of promoting internal cohesion. "As Christianity came to terms with the Roman Empire, highly centralized and bureaucratic especially since the reforms of Diocletian (284–305), the old loose organization of the Church had to accommodate itself to political realities. The demands for uniformity were inexorable. It was the Emperor Constantine himself who summoned the first Ecumenical Council, pressured the participants to come to agreement, and enforced the decisions. It was this Council of Nicaea in 325 that canonized a superstructure, the metropolitanate and the beginnings of a patriarchal system."[5] Constantine the convert thus became Constantine the controller, shaping the organizational structure of the Church to suit his needs. Centralization proceeded apace.

[5] Lynch, *op. cit.*, p. 3.

If the merger with the Empire strengthened the papacy, so did the Empire's collapse. The weakness of Rome around A.D. 400 created new uncertainty and threat, but this time for the population at large. The Romans were terrified as the emperors proved helpless to stop the attacks of the Visigoths and the Huns. When Pope Leo the Great persuaded Attila to spare Rome, the prestige of the papacy increased dramatically. In fact, "the position of the papacy was so strengthened by Leo that it was able to survive the fall of the West–Roman Empire (476) without difficulty".[6] For well over a century the popes exerted strong secular leadership to reduce the continuing threats. Gregory the Great (590–604) organized the land holdings of the Church to increase the crop yield, distributed grain to the peasants suffering under the barbarian invasions, provided military protection and otherwise emerged as a major temporal leader. This combination of external attacks and a secular leadership vacuum further contributed to the centralization of the Church, with the pope now emerging as commander-in-chief as well as pontiff.

But time and again the marriage of *regnum* and *sacerdotium* was to prove troublesome. The symbiosis of Church and State in the feudal period produced new threats to papal authority, and new attempts to defend it. The most grave danger was temporal encroachment on ecclesiastical power through lay investiture. Rising to the defence of the Church's rights of appointment, Pope Gregory VII issued his famous *Dictatus Papae* (1075) in which he argued that the pope was the supreme head of Christianity, standing above kings and emperors. This brought him into direct confrontation with Henry IV in a sequence too well known to review here. The Gregorian reforms, however, went well beyond Canossa, and brought on a sharp increase in the power and authority of the pope. Gregory established a system of papal legates which provided an effective vehicle for information-gathering as well as centralized direction. Moreover, "appellations to the Holy See increased, especially in the case of contested episcopal elections, and supplied the pope with the opportunity to intervene directly in the dioceses.... After the eleventh century the metropolitans had to go to Rome personally to obtain

[6] A. Franzen, revised and edited by John Dolan, *A Concise History of the Church* (New York, 1969), p. 105.

their staffs, and after the twelfth century they had to swear a special oath of obedience and appear in Rome periodically (every four years) for the *visitatio liminum apostolorum*."[7] The emerging pattern was clear: an escalation of decision-making to the office and the person of the pope. Gregory's vision of papal primacy was fully realized under Innocent III (1198–1216).

The period following Innocent saw a drastic curtailment of the temporal power of the papacy, and a fresh crisis of authority. In a pattern to be repeated in 1870, Boniface VIII responded to a loss of *regnum* by attempting to fortify the teaching authority of the papacy. In the bull *Unam Sanctam* (1302) he declared obedience to the pope necessary for salvation. After his death there was a marked reaction against the excesses of papalism, reinforced by the Babylonian captivity, and conciliarism became the order of the day. In striking contrast to *Unam Sanctam*, the Council of Constance, in its decree *Haec Sancta* (1415), established that all Christians, even the pope, must be obedient to the councils. Ironically, the net effect of this decree was less to promote conciliarism than to create a lingering threat for succeeding popes. As Franzen writes, "... the effects of conciliarism were to be felt for a long time, and fear of its revival governed the popes from this time on".[8] Their sense of the future may have been misguided, but their memory of the past was clear.

IV. THE REFORMATION TO 1870

The Reformation brought on the most serious environmental crisis ever facing the Church. The reformers' attacks hit precisely on matters having to do with centralization and authority. The notions of a priesthood of all believers and justification by faith alone directly challenged the position that truth was centrally mediated through the successor of Peter. Not surprisingly, the Council of Trent responded by reinforcing those elements mostly directly under siege—the priesthood and the hierarchical structure of authority.

Several specific steps taken at Trent and in the Counter-Reformation greatly enhanced the strength of the papacy. For one, the

[7] *Ibid.*, p. 184.   [8] *Ibid.*, p. 244.

Council fathers entrusted the work of reform to the pope, and supplied him with a mandate to clean the house. This very action increased the salience and prestige of the papacy, which had been flagging. Pius V (1566–1572) rose to the challenge by instituting a major overhaul of the Church's administrative structures. His first task was to purge corrupt elements from the college of cardinals, which he then gave major responsibility for internal reforms. He also established the Congregation for the Propagation of the Faith, and ordered visitations and synods throughout the Church to ensure compliance with the reforms. One of his most far-reaching accomplishments was to rejuvenate the Roman Curia and transform it into an efficient administrative arm. The revitalized Curia, for its part, began to intervene more and more in the internal affairs of countries and dioceses. Its contribution to centralization was bolstered by the establishment of papal nunciatures. In the crisis atmosphere following the Reformation the nuncios became not only foreign representatives of the papacy, but also independent reporters and intelligence agents monitoring the obedience and loyalty of local clergy. Because of their volume and sensitivity, the reports from the nunciatures created new demands for information-handling capability and centralization in Rome. Eventually the rising power of the nuncios, mirroring the strength of the papacy, set off counter-reactions, such as Gallicanism and Febronianism, which argued for national autonomy. These threats reinforced the will of the popes to maintain and expand their centralized power.

Beginning with the French Revolution and continuing through 1870, the secular power of the Church came under constant attack. Uncertainty and threat were not confined to the environment of the Church. The chaos and violence of the Revolution and the Napoleonic wars left a wake of anxiety and turmoil in the European population as a whole. The convergence of an attack on the Church and distress in the secular environment once again turned the spotlight on the See of Peter. Many "... sought haven in a Church which to them appeared to offer security in a world whose foundations were crumbling. The currents which made for secularization and de-Christianization were still potent, but the counter-currents were rising and were stronger than they had been since the seventeenth century".[9] Writers such as De Maistre and Lamennais began to portray the papacy as the only remaining bulwark of order. As the secularizing-nationalist movements gained ground in the nineteenth century, many backward-looking monarchists and representatives of besieged national churches joined the chorus.

By mid-century the *resorgimento* posed an immediate threat to the papal states. In a massive effort at equilibration of authority, Pius IX took steps to enlarge his jurisdiction and influence in other areas. One move was the further centralization of administrative control in Rome. Questions of liturgy, discipline and appointments were increasingly decided by the pope and the Curia. In addition, Pius IX both encouraged and accommodated the movement towards a personal veneration of the pope through audiences, blessings and pilgrimages. During the same period he supported the re-establishment of Peter's Pence as a voluntary offering for the pope and Curia and encouraged the flow of young Catholics into the papal armies. To quote Cozemius, "This was the climate in which it began to seem as if the strengthening of papal authority was the alpha and omega of ecclesiastical wisdom."[10] Set in this context, the definition of the Immaculate Conception in 1854 could be seen as an added attempt to strengthen the teaching authority of the pope at a time when his secular power was evaporating.

The crowning triumph of papalization was, of course, the definition of infallibility in 1870. Pius called the Vatican Council in 1869 in an atmosphere of extreme political apprehension, if not panic. The wolf, in the flesh of Victor Emmanuel II, was at the door. Whatever the doctrinal merits of the matter, the definition of papal infallibility at this juncture was an adroit political move. "But would anyone venture to proceed against a pope whose universal primacy and personal infallibility had been solemnly and definitively proclaimed *urbi et orbi* in an ecumenical council? This was almost the sole ray of hope for those who fought... for the maintenance of the papal states."[11] The intro-

[9] K. S. Latourette, *Christianity in a Revolutionary Age, I, The Nineteenth Century in Europe* (New York, 1958), p. 238.

[10] V. Cozemius, quoted in H. Küng, *Infallible? An Inquiry* (Garden City, New York, 1971), p. 128.

[11] *Ibid.*, pp. 91–2.

duction to the constitution *Pastor Aeternus* leaves little doubt about the role of uncertainty and threat in this definition: "With daily increasing hatred, on all sides, the gates of hell are rising, to overturn the Church if it were possible, against its divinely established foundation."[12] The fall of Rome in 1870 and the subsequent "imprisonment" of the pope in the Vatican only served to reinforce the defensive posture of the papacy, and to increase the demands for centralization. The basic structure of formal authority left by Pius IX has continued with only minor modifications until the present time. In fact, by a curious process the pope has become the prisoner of his own infallibility.

This discussion suggests a strong tendency towards the conservation of authority in the interactions between the Church and its changing environments. Losses on one front, such as temporal power, give rise to fortifications and often gains in others. In these responses the Church and the popes show marked similarities to organizations and leaders pursuing very different goals. On the basis of this preliminary review, it would appear that much can be learned by the systematic comparison of the Church and other organizations.

[12] *Ibid.*, pp. 94-5.

Thomas O'Dea

Pathology and Renewal of Religious Institutions

THE phenomena which typically exhibit the pathology of institutions are in fact exaggerated forms of normal strains and tensions. Order, though necessary, tends too often to be purchased at the price of routinization. Goal achievement requires goal specification, a process that is unavoidably historically conditioned and therefore involves covert though substantial elements of goal displacement. Motivational engagement, a functional prerequisite, leads under specific societal conditions to an involvement of vested interests which rigidifies existing stabilities and stands in the way of reform and renewal. These are some aspects of the perennial tension between stability and creativity characteristic of institutional life.[1]

Two perennial pitfalls with respect to them should be avoided. The first is to see institutions as simply constraints and as extrinsic interferences with the life of the spirit. The second is to fail to recognize the seriousness of the tensions that exist between the spirit and the institutional pathways it has created in the past. The former finds expression in all those doctrines of the "invisible" Church for whom "to worship God in spirit and in truth" requires a utopian absence of institutionalization, for whom man, though born free, is everywhere in institutional chains. The latter is to be seen in that kind of "ecclesiolatry" which forgets that established ecclesial forms are not only "ways"

[1] For a detailed treatment from another perspective see Thomas F. O'Dea, "Five Dilemmas in the Institutionalization of Religion", in *Sociology and the Study of Religion* (New York, 1970), pp. 240–55.

but pre-eminently "ways to"—ways to the divine-human relationship, and that they can be transformed by history into obstacles in its way.

A typical consequence of institutional pathology is that it obscures the line—difficult enough to identify—between the essential and accidental and tends to exalt what *is* as the best possible expression of what *ought to be*. It becomes an obstacle in the way of the vitally necessary process of continual clarification of man's on-going religious experience.

I. Tension between Two Vocations

Every society is an acted out answer to the implicit question, what ought man to be doing here below, being the kind of being that he is? It is an answer acted out under the press of circumstance and hence highly conditioned both in form and content. It is an open-ended drama that actualizes selective aspects of man's polymorphous endowment. Central to it has been the acting out of a religious relationship. In the past societies were generally sacral entities, within which men acted out their answers to the constitutive question in forms that were at once "worldly" and "religious". Life was a quasi-sacramental phenomenon as may be seen in the archaic empires of the East from ancient Egypt to eighteenth-century China. Israel and Greece broke out of this "enchanted garden", to use Weber's phrase, and these breakthroughs proved constitutive of a new kind of attitude towards nature and tradition. Greek man discovered himself to be a being of whose vocation knowing was constitutive— a rational being related to transcendent reason. In the Old Testament, on the other hand, man saw himself called to an ethical relationship and to one of fellowship with God who transcended the world. Immersed in the here and now, he found himself called by something beyond. He was, in Jaspers' term, a "boundary phenomenon", simultaneously elicited by two vocations.

Man had a worldly vocation to increase and multiply and subdue the earth and replenish it, and a religious vocation to love the Lord God with all his soul, mind and strength. Not necessarily contradictory, the two presented grounds for conflict, as may be seen in the encounter of Samuel and Saul, and more dramatically in Jeremiah. Within Israel, these two vocations remained concretized in a single covenant community, though tension between them was evident. The Church became a new Israel, the Pauline divine commonwealth or the earthly embodiment of Augustine's City of God. It became the institutional expression of the religious vocation. Other institutions, though necessary and legitimate, were seen as residual.

The Church saw man called to a theocentric vocation as a member of a christocentric community. So great was the impact of this call that the early Church had to argue to defend the legitimacy of earthly callings. Conditioned by its social situation the Church transformed the indifference of the gospel to the world into contempt and hostility. The Church played the anomalous role of receiving, nurturing and transmitting ancient culture, while it never fully recognized the worldly vocation. Martyrdom and celibacy symbolized its basic stand. Monasticism became the practical expression of the Catholic vocation and provided the highest answer to the constitutive question. Moreover, the semi-barbarous conditions of worldly life in the early Middle Ages enhanced the appeal of the cloister and further obscured the value of the secular.

In early medieval society, the worldly vocation found expression chiefly in the activities of ruling classes. Later on, economic and intellectual developments would provide attractive spheres of lay activity. The Church's attitude towards such developments was varied, often ambiguous, and often dictated by institutional vested interests. It both sponsored and constrained such developments as may be seen in the case of the university. The Church's religious vocation and its historically conditioned view of lay life made it undervalue secular activity in terms of spiritual seriousness and moral worth. Its vested interests often placed it in institutional competition with secular pursuits. Vested interests, an historically conditioned definition of the religious life, and the interests of the institution as a functioning entity obscured recognition of the true problem, the inevitable conflict between man's two legitimate callings.

The postponement of the *parousia* and the development of the Church as a mediational institution tended to make history less real for later Christians. History's end had really been accomplished and we but awaited its full manifestation. In this view, the work of the world, the second vocation, became relatively unimportant.

The victory of the Church over the Empire in the Investiture struggle and the confrontation with the Hohenstaufen assured the independence of the Church, although the issue continually reasserted itself. It also prevented the emergence of a viable Christian Empire. Such an entity would have been ambiguous, for it would to some extent have represented a consolidation of the archaic relation of men to tradition and to nature, but it would also have granted a fuller legitimation to lay life. These struggles set the stage for modern developments, since they placed the Church in opposition, seeing other vocations as competitive rather than complementary. The legitimation of lay vocations would have involved a large measure of revolt. This process came to a head first in the development of science which was experienced as threatening. Thus the modern embodiment of the Greek breakthrough achieved its liberty as an anti-religious phenomenon. It came to a head politically in the French Revolution which proclaimed a new holy community and offered a rival doctrine of salvation. Hence the twin dramas of the nineteenth-century struggle of science versus religion, and the Revolution versus the Church.

It is against this background that the operation of the typical pathology of institutions must be understood. The Church not only failed to grasp the true thrust of modern developments and opposed them. Its own specific forms of the religious vocation also became hardened and rigid. The religious life itself was suffering from institutional truncation. Its forms were becoming alienated and the Church tended to resort to authority in compensation.

II. Loss of Plausibility for Religion

Thus the stage was set for the two great historical secessions, a secular one to assert the value of the worldly vocation and a religious one to free the religious vocation from institutionalized constraints. In the first, the "various priesthoods of second causes rose against the alienation of their domain into the hands of the priesthood of the First Cause".[2] The second, actually beginning earlier than Luther, eventually divided the Church. Its first major consequence was to sweep "away such beginnings of a free and secular civilization as had already been toilsomely established". Its long range and lasting effect, produced "indirectly" and "against its will", was to sustain and hasten the process of secularization.[3] Thus developed what Tillich called "autonomous civilization" in the West, making the religious vocation residual and rendering both institutionally confined and experientially distorted.

What evolved here, whether in Whig, revolutionary, bourgeois or technocratic forms, was the centrality of the worldly vocation, together with the increasing residuality of the religious vocation, whether embodied in Church, sect or denomination. These developments involved genuine innovation. They signified and realized nothing less than a new relation of man to nature (technology and mastery) and a new relation of man to institutions— those crystallized embodiments of the experience and value-judgments of the past. Towards each, modern Western man has evolved a novel independence, an unprecedented autonomy. He no longer feels himself a part of nature or a part of his group and its past in the same way as his ancestors did before the eighteenth century. A hitherto undeveloped human possibility has come to the fore. Man has not come of age—Bonhoeffer was premature about that—but he has left his ancestral home. This modern venture is both challenging and upsetting. To face it with responsible creativity is not easy. For many it raised the spectre of nihilism and the threat of meaninglessness. This new possibility of personal openness and responsibility as the basis of growth as well as the risks it unavoidably involves, were based in their emergence upon biblical religion. It was the religious vocation which provided, to use Parsons' expression, the Archimedean point for the achievement of personal autonomy.[4] Relation to

[2] Yves M. J. Congar, *Lay People in the Church* (Westminster, Md., 1957), p. 33.

[3] Ernst Troeltsch, *Protestantism and Progress: A Historical Study of the Relation of Protestantism to the Modern World* (New York, 1912), pp. 85-7.

[4] Talcott Parsons, *The Structure of Social Action* (Glencoe, Ill., 1949), p. 549, and J. J. Mol, *The Breaking of Traditions* (Berkeley, 1968).

transcendence was the basis of exodus from the "enchanted garden" of archaism; its methodology was that of rationality. Yet this new view of his world and himself led Western man when confronted with earlier evolved forms of the religious vocation to abandon traditional religion. Here again the pathology of institutions exacerbated the severity of the problem. As a consequence both an activist penultimate prometheanism and a variety of nostalgias for archaism characterize the mentalities of our time.

The religious vocation lost plausibility and resonance for the new mentality because the forms in which it presented itself seemed obsolete—they were forms which still emphasized traditional submission to nature and tradition. New embodiments of the religious vocation recognizing the legitimate claim of the new existential stance of modernity did not develop sufficiently to reorganize the religious life and render it contemporary. The one modern innovation of note, the denominational form of religious fellowship, tended under the circumstances to embody not only individual autonomy but also cultural residuality.

III. The New Religious Quest

The centrality of the secular and the residuality of the religious vocation was characteristic of life in America, when, in the nineteen-sixties after two world wars, the successful development of scientific technology, and the development of a pluralist society, the nineteenth century finally came to an end. This end was symbolized by a great change in American Catholic life, a change that found expression in the election of a Catholic to the Presidency and somewhat later the prominence of Catholics in radical protest. The new relation of man to nature and tradition was becoming the common property of Catholics. A Catholic President announced the plan to put an American on the moon and Catholic priests broke the law to bear witness to conscience. Moreover, the loss of religious conviction among many of the secular introduced a period of seeking and experimenting—often with bizarre forms of religion. Max Weber had thought that modern society had needed its religious foundation only to undergird its origin, but that once in existence it would run autonomously and automatically.[5] He proved to be wrong. Americans found their sons and daughters engaged in a quest for meaning, a search for community, a seeking after vocation. Despite the ubiquitousness of irresponsibility—innocent and otherwise, despite the longing for archaism, despite even a turn to traditional religion in looking for reality and meaning, the fact remains that a return to older forms is not really possible. For a long time the Catholic Church felt with Pius IX that modern man had taken the wrong road. For a long time it saw him as a prodigal son and called and prayed for him to return to his Father's house. It overlooked the fact that all houses are provisional, that in the deeper sense we are all strangers and sojourners here below and that man is an historical being who cannot really go home again.

A recognition of the necessity of institutions, of the strategic importance of community and tradition, must also involve a recognition of their perennial pathology. It is the function of the religious institution to provide the shared basis for the divine-human encounter and relationship. That involves developing forms of thought, liturgy and organization for the expression and acting out, the definition and comprehension so far as they may be defined and comprehended, of this encounter and relationship. Such developments necessarily involve relativizing the absolute. But the pathology of institutions, a fundamentalism about behavioural and intellectual specifications and concretizations, a tendency to transform means into ends, and the investment of self-interested motivation in existing forms, together with a fear of openness that derives from the very ontological frailty of faith—all these transform the relativizing of the absolute into the absolutizing of the relative.[6]

Christianity has experienced two massive attempts to renew and reformulate its life and thought in order to make the Christian relationship to God in Christ a viable option for modern man. The first was made by liberal Protestantism whose gains

[5] Max Weber, *The Protestant Ethic and the Spirit of Capitalism* (New York and London), pp. 181–2.

[6] On the ontological and therefore sociological weakness of faith see Eric Voegelin, *The New Science of Politics* (Chicago and London, 1952), p. 122.

were authentic but which often tended to lose the transcendental insight and relation themselves. The second came slowly and against enormous institutional resistance within Roman Catholicism and moved onto open ground with Vatican II. It too registered real breakthrough, but it let lose forces making both for growth and for disorganization and irresponsibility. The protective maturity of the constraining institution proved when once removed to have been a cloak concealing considerable religious immaturity. Today the issue is joined and the challenge remains. How is the Church to make constitutive for Christian life the Johannine fellowship of the sons of God in faith and the Pauline liberty of the Christian? How to do so and at the same time relate the religious calling to the secular vocation of modern man?

Today the secular vocation means making the earth liveable. It involves the advance of knowledge, the stimulation of culture and the promotion of a level of general welfare commensurable with resources and technology. Man's fulfilment requires the harmonious development of both vocations. Modern man is not called upon to become a one-sided Prometheus who "hates all gods" (Marx made the phrase his own!). Nor is he necessarily destined to fall back into neo-archaisms—a fall that could entail catastrophe of a kind of which the nineteen-thirties and forties gave us a foretaste. Rather modern man is called to nurture within himself the image and likeness of God while performing responsibly his worldly tasks in co-operation with the creator in the unfinished work of the creation.

What all this implies of course is that today the implicit constitutive question—What ought man to be doing here below, being the kind of being that he is?—now arises in consciousness in urgent if often confused form. How can the Church receive this question and contribute to the clarification of the tasks it implies? The Church must preserve tradition without absolutizing the relative. Only thus can it provide the necessary meaningful context and protect the requisite openness at the same time. How can the Church preserve community in this interim period of profound transformation without rigidifying its forms so as to provide both the nurture of fellowship and the openness necessary for authentic growth? These are the questions of today and neither the anxieties that arise from the natural frailty of faith nor the pathologies that unavoidably attend institutional life must be allowed to inhibit our facing and grappling with them. For the fact is that man will find his way to fulfilment not by a return to the "enchanted garden" that surrounded the ancestral estate, but by human fellowship in relation to that God who is within, above, and before him in his earthly pilgrimage—that God in whom our hearts may rest whatever be the turmoil, since he is God.

Richard Guerrette

The Re-Identity of the Priest: An Organizational Solution

ONE of the most helpful studies that have been conducted on the identity crisis in the priesthood in the post-conciliar Church has been that of two organizational scientists at Yale University, Douglas T. Hall and Benjamin Schneider. Having carefully examined the work experiences and career growth of a cross-section of priests of a large diocese on the eastern coast of the United States, their research exposed the underlying organizational causes of the crisis and indicated the need for the Church to be responsive and adaptive to its internal systems and to the external environment for the purpose of resolving the crisis. This article represents an attempt to indicate how the Church can provide such an organizational solution to the crisis and thus offer the priest adequate institutional resources for his re-identity in the ministry. First, a brief account of the conclusions of the Yale study will be rendered and then, by applying some sociological theory to ecclesiology, an analysis will be made of the internal system problems of the Church which fix the organizational setting for the identity crisis in the priesthood. Finally, a sociological plan for the pastoral reform of the Church will be submitted as a means for enabling the Church to respond and to be adaptive to its internal systems and to the external environment with a view to resolving the crisis for the priest through the agility of its own institutional resources.

I. The Yale Study

By measuring the correlates of personal growth and organizational effectiveness among the participating priests, Hall and Schneider showed that curates (assistant pastors) possessed a very low level of individual development in their work and that this problem was directly related to the type of authority that they experienced. These researchers presented data which attested to a serious under-utilization of skills on the part of the curates, critical dissatisfaction in their work and poor self-perception from their superior-subordinate relationships. By analysing the actual work assignments of these priests, Hall and Schneider further showed that the possibilities for career growth in the present organizational system of the Church were scarce. They revealed that these work assignments repeatedly inhibited the psychological success of the curates and that such inhibitions in their personal growth process caused cyclical interruptions in their career development. These Yale scientists traced the organizational causes of these problems of role identity in the priesthood to the following factors: (1) the curates possessed extremely limited opportunities for goal challenge and work choice and almost no opportunities for receiving feedback on their work performance; (2) while few of them could claim the independence of working autonomously, even fewer enjoyed supportive autonomy from their pastors; (3) they were frequently engaged in work not central to their concept of ministry; and (4) in such a work climate the possibilities for the attainment of their goals were considerably diminished.[1]

The work of Hall and Schneider suggests quite imperatively that resolving the identity crisis in the priesthood is basically a matter of reforming the institutional resources of parish structures in order to create more productive organizational conditions in the Church and more satisfactory authority relationships in the ministry. In this kind of work climate where the priest can enjoy personal development and organizational effectiveness and

---

[1] D. Hall and B. Schneider, *A Study of Work Experiences and Career Growth of Roman Catholic Diocesan Priests* (unpublished manuscript), Department of Administrative Sciences, Yale University (New Haven, 1969), pp. 54–116.

where he can experience psychological success and career growth, he will perceive sufficient competence in his self-image as to acquire the necessary motivation not only for his re-identity in the ministry but also for his continuing development in its profession.

II. Sociological Theory and Ecclesiology

Creating such a favourable work climate in the organizational system of the Church requires the interdisciplinary task of applying some sociological theory to ecclesiology. This method of resolving the identity crisis in the priesthood can be effective since, in addition to analysing the system problems of the Church, it can provide an actual sociological plan for the integrative reform of parish structures in which setting more productive organizational conditions could be created and more collegial authority relationships established. The need to apply sociological theory to ecclesiology is pronounced not exclusively by the personnel problems in the priesthood pressing for structural change but also by the pathological problems in the Church provoked by cultural change. This latter set of problems, rather malignant with institutional conflict, infests the organizational system of the Church and not only polarizes the priesthood but also threatens the very foundations of ecclesial unity.

Inasmuch as the sociological theories of Talcott Parsons, the distinguished American sociologist, address themselves to the functional problems of differentiation in organizational systems, these theories are quite well-suited to analyse the system problems of the Church and to draw a sociological plan for its pastoral reform which is equipped to resolve the polarizing conflicts in the priesthood and to promote institutional unity. According to Parsons, the organizational conflicts of any institution can be adequately resolved by respecting "four independent functional imperatives: *adaptation, goal-attainment, integration* and *latency.*

In order to explicate these functional imperatives, it is important to understand how Parsons explains the sources of organizational conflict. While an organization is maintained according to an institutionalized value system, its values are continually subject to change because of external and internal forces. The external forces are those which originate from outside cultural influences and exert pressure on the organization to change its value system. The internal forces are those which originate from inside motivational tensions and exert pressure among the members to rebel against particular institutionalized role expectations. As the two primary sources of organizational conflict, these forces challenge the very stability of an institution in terms of its "pattern maintenance" (structures) and its "tension management" (authority). Wherefore, the most conserving functional imperative for the organizational stability of an institution is latency. In the stress of these system problems generated by these forces of change, the organization's efficiency is impeded and its institutional unity imperilled. As the functional imperative for relaxing these strains, integration preserves solidarity among the diversified membership and promotes operational efficiency. Adaptation is the functional imperative which deals with the system problems caused by the organization's interchange with the external environment and enables the institution to adjust to the process of differentiation as it encounters change. The function of goal-attainment permits the organization to control the environment by manœuvring among particular situational conditions with a strategy for economic gratification. This sociological theory of Persons, usually signified as his AGIL scheme, indicates how an organization can maintain equilibrium through its own institutional resources and ensure its continued existence and growth through the use of these four functional imperatives in spite of its organizational conflicts.[2]

Applying this sociological theory to ecclesiology, it is possible to interpret the organizational conflicts of the Church in terms of its eschatological nature and its missionary purpose. The AGIL scheme of Parsons can set the perimeters for this interpretation and can thus outline how the Church can resolve these conflicts through *structural adaptation, goal substitution* and *integration* with respect for its *latent religious values*. Inasmuch as this interpretation of Parsons' scheme can assess the internal system problems of the organizational Church and can measure its adaptive capacity to respond to the external environment, it per-

[2] T. Parsons, *Economy and Society* (Glencoe, Ill., 1956), pp. 16–19.

mits the Church to invert the functional imperative of changing the environment to meet the needs of the system, as Parsonian theory would dictate,[3] and to re-order its institutional priorities by changing the system to meet the needs of the environment, as conciliar theology would indicate.[4] The Church, unlike the secular institutions of society which are dependent upon economic gratification for the attainment of their goals, exists for the dis- interested missionary service of society and is dependent upon salvific gratification for the attainment of its goals. To this end, it operates according to the principle of adaptation[5] and therefore must change its system, whenever necessary, to include the sub- stitution of more immediate practical goals, particularly when these substituted goals would help to save human lives as well as human souls. In this process, it also operates according to the principle of integration and therefore must preserve institutional unity amid functional diversity, as it conserves its traditional religious values.[6] By so employing the four functional imperatives in order to resolve its system problems, the Church can indeed acquire a more transcendent social identity and yet function as a more productive organizational entity.[7]

III. A Sociological Analysis of the System Problems

With the application of the above sociological theory to ecclesi- ology, a functional analysis of the system problems of the insti- tutional Church can now be made in order to define the organizational setting which is provoking the identity crisis in the priesthood. By using the Parsonian scheme, the analysis should expose the conflicting tensions which are polarizing the priesthood and dividing the Church.

[3] T. Parsons, *Sociological Theory and Modern Society* (New York, 1967), p. 493.
[4] Pastoral Constitution, *Gaudium et Spes*, on the Church in the Modern World, 44 and 76.
[5] *Ibid.*, 44, footnote 146 in W. Abbott, ed., *The Documents of Vatican II* (New York, 1966), p. 246.
[6] *Ibid.*, 92.
[7] This use of Parsons' scheme is more consistent with the critique of his theory by G. Winter in *Elements for a Social Ethic* (New York, 1966), pp. 206-8.

As traditional parish structures tend to contain the Church within the confines of its own parochial interests, Christians possessing wider social concerns feel the need to adapt these structures in order to maximize the Church's relationship to the external environment and to mobilize its resources for the missionary goals of serving the distressed of society. Because of the economic strain and the institutional weight of the parochial form of the parish and its self-containing goals, perceiving Christians tend to question the values of their attainment. As these people become more aware of the secular implications of the Church's mission and more sensitive to human suffering and want, they are beginning to substitute more immediate goals that are capable of responding to the urgency of a situation.

Threatened by these new forms of structural adaptation and by their old fears of secularized goals, conserving Christians tend to stabilize into their protective congregations in order to preserve their latent religious values. Fearful of losing the continuity of tradition and the security of their identity, they are suspicious of Church renewal. The "pattern maintenance" function of the traditional form of the parish and the "tension management" function of the expected role of the priest relax these fears and protect these Christians from the external influences of cultural change and the internal pressures of motivational unrest.

Sensitive to the organizational problems provoked by the forces of change and to the consequent conflicts of institutional disharmony, moderate Christians are intent to work within the system for their response to change, committed to preserve the unity of the Church and to ensure its effectiveness in mission. Although they may be in the best position to bring about solidarity and efficiency in the institutional Church through their integrative efforts, they are seriously handicapped by a need for a sustained and systematic plan for responding to change and by a resultant lack of direction from the hierarchy.

From this brief analysis of the system problems of the Church, one can almost feel the institutional tensions in the organizational setting of parish structures which bind the priest into his expected parochial role. In so far as these tensions remain unrelaxed, the priest will continue to be restricted to such institutionalized role expectations. With no scientific plan for an integrative response to these system problems, the priest will be considerably inhibited from assuming any innovative roles in adapted structures that would contribute to his personal growth and career development. It is conclusively clear, then, that such a plan is acutely needed if the very admonitions of Vatican II regarding contemporary forms of ministry are to be faithfully heeded: "All (priests) indeed are united in the single goal of building up Christ's Body, a work requiring manifold roles and new adjustments, especially nowadays."[8]

IV. A Sociological Plan for Pastoral Reform

By continuing to employ the Parsonian scheme, it is possible to outline a sociological plan for pastoral reform from which manifold roles could be developed for the priest to enable him to make the necessary adjustments for ministry in the contemporary world. As this plan is constructed to resolve the system problems of differentiation in the institutional Church analysed above, it is equipped not only to depolarize the priesthood but to unite the whole Church in the common work of building up the Body of Christ. By providing alternative parish forms through which this missionary work can be organized in accordance with the functional imperatives of Parsons' theory, the plan should unfold integrative pastoral settings in which more productive organizational conditions could be constituted and more collegial authority relationships established.

1. *Structural Adaptation.* New models of Christian community could be designed along the functional lines of structural adaptation in order to expand the missionary activity of the Church beyond the parochial enclosures of traditional forms. Liberated from territorial confinement, these innovative forms would be so adapted to a mobilized society as to allow Christian fellowship to be expressed as a "way" of life (Ac. 9. 2; 24. 12, 22) in accordance with contemporary environmental factors. Multiple structural forms, such as the floating parish, the *oikos* (household) commune, the Pentecostal community, the hospice, the

---

[8] Decree on the Ministry and Life of Priests, 8 (*W. Abbott*).

servant storefront, the ecumenical parish, etc., would maximize the Church's relationship to society and would mobilize its ministerial resources to include in its missionary work force the baptized faithful as well as the ordained priest.

2. *Goal Substitution.* Other innovative models of Christian community designed for the functional purposes of goal substitution could enable the Church to deepen its involvement in the social order. By judiciously adopting certain ideologies from such out-ward-orientated movements as the civil rights movement, the peace movement, the youth movement, the citizens' action move-ment and the liberation movements and by theologically en-dorsing them with a faith commitment for a self-sacrificing gospel service to humanity, these communal forms could be more meaningful signs of hope in the eternal to those struggling in the despair of the present. They could also be constituted as exemplary signs to other institutions of society, announcing that, as communities of God's people in the organizational Church, they are committed to the reconciliatory task of changing its system to meet the needs of the people. By so expressing their witness in the socio-political context of mission, these prophetic forms of parish community could serve society with well-effected compassion and thus give individuals more immediate access to the wholeness of life.

3. *Latent Religious Values.* By utilizing the functional impera-tive of latency for the purpose of conserving the religious values of tradition, the Church could preserve the basic form of the territorial parish and stabilize the traditional role of the parish priest. Because of the diversity of the other forms of parish out-lined in this plan and the multiplicity of the other roles of min-istry to be developed in its implementation, the local parish would become smaller and more communal through more serviceable structures of inter- and intra-parochial communication and colla-boration in the apostolate. By so avoiding the narrow enclosures of parochialism, this form would no longer pathologically con-fine the people and the priest to the latency of the static values of tradition but would protectively define them in the security of historical continuity and social cohesion for their creative and collaborative response to cultural and religious change.

4. *Integration*. As the keystone to organizational unity, integrative models of Christian community could be designed to secure institutional solidarity and operational efficiency in the Church. Supportive to the structures of the more innovative forms of parish community coexisting within the areas of their own territorial limits, some patterns of the traditional type of local parish reformed into smaller sectional parishes, co-pastorates and team parishes would consolidate the membership of the local (diocesan) Church and conjoin its ministerial work. These forms would create the organizational conditions through which bishops, priests and all the faithful, liberals and conservatives alike, could efficiently collaborate in their common missionary task of building up the Body of Christ. Finally, these forms would establish the structural lines through which the hierarchical authority of the Church could be more collegially expressed in accordance with the organizational principle of superior co-ordination.[9]

5. *Re-identity through Personal Development and Career Growth*. With the emergence of these integrative pastoral settings through the implementation of the above sociological plan for pastoral reform, the proper organizational conditions in the Church would be so created and authentic collegial authority relationships so established as to enable the priest to re-identify in the ministry. The organizational conditions laid out in this plan and the authority relationships demanded by the functional imperatives of its design would form an institutional base for a work climate in which the priest would possess abundant opportunities for goal challenge and work choice. With the diversity in communal forms and the multiplicity in ministerial roles, the priest could set preferred goals for himself in accordance with his personal charisms and his professional interests and, with the aid of a personnel board and the approval of the bishop, select a

[9] This integrative expression of episcopal authority from Parsonian organizational theory affirms the function of superior co-ordination as imperative for hierarchical institutions. Cf. C. Morse, "The Functional Imperatives", *The Social Theories of Talcott Parsons*, ed., M. Black (Englewood Cliffs, N.J., 1961), pp. 121, 151-2. It also reflects the biblical paradigm of the bishop's supervisory role of administrative overseer in the primitive Church. Cf. R. Brown, *Priest and Bishop: Biblical Reflections* (New York, 1970), pp. 37-8 and 67-8.

suitable assignment where he could work to attain them. In these assignments, he could have access to channels for collective feedback in his work through review boards of regional or parish councils.[10]

With authority relationships renewed by the conciliar principle of collegiality and the organizational principle of superior co-ordination, he would be assured of enjoying a considerable amount of autonomy in his work along with the supportive interest of his superiors. Finally, with more opportunities for community involvement and personal development through his preferred work assignments (criteria which curates ranked in the Yale study as very important on their priority list of work activities), the priest would be increasingly engaged in work that is central to his concept of ministry and relevant to his self-image perception.[11] In this kind of organizational system where the priest would utilize his skills and so realize self-actualization as well as promotional recognition, he would enjoy deep satisfaction in his work and acquire adequate self-perception through his roles. In this kind of organizational Church where the priest would thus steadily advance to a high level of personal development in his profession, he would experience sufficient psychological success and achieve proportionate career growth as to ensure continuing development in his ministerial identity.

By way of summary and conclusion, the organizational studies of Hall and Schneider and the sociological theories of Talcott Parsons offer the Church an interdisciplinary base for the construction of a systematic plan to resolve the identity crisis in the priesthood in terms of its own institutional resources. If conciliar theology can define the contemporary need for "manifold roles and new adjustments" for the integrity of the priesthood, the

[10] This process would restore the right of the community, which the priest is called to serve, to test his service, a right which is founded on the charism of discernment (1 Cor. 12. 10). Cf. H. Küng, *The Church* (London and New York, 1967), pp. 421–2 and 440.

[11] Cultivating an acute awareness of a functional identity for the priest through a relevant self-image dimension is not simply a practical application of good organizational theory to the problems of professional ministry but a pastoral conclusion of current process thought for their resolutions. Cf. N. Pittenger, *The Christian Church as Social Process* (Philadelphia, 1971), pp. 97 and 117.

above scientific theories on institutional forms and the suggested sociological plan for pastoral reform can design these roles and assign these adjustments for the re-identity of the priest. The application of these organizational theories to ecclesiology and the implementation of the plan would help the Church to know and the priest to experience that the interdependent forms of parish and roles of ministry possess ecclesiological stability and promote priestly identity through institutional AGILity.

L. Vaskovics

Theses on the Interdependence of Religious Organizations and Familial Sub-Systems

THE interdependence of religious organization and familial systems was not a central research topic among earlier sociologists of religion. The interaction of these two social phenomena did not appear to be problematic. In the teaching of the Christian churches, the family was not only the basic unit of society but also the basic model for ecclesiastical organization (e.g., the patriarchal role structure). As the smallest "natural" element of the ecclesiastical organization, the family had specific functions. It was the most important area of religious activity and the most important point of transmission of Church values, attitudes and actions. This superstructure of ecclesiastical functions also seemed natural until comparative cultural anthropology and ethnology revealed how varied religious organizations and family structures were. The awareness of these findings has made the question of the interdependence of religious organizations and families more urgent, although it has not as yet produced a clear theoretical or empirical analysis.

The religious function of the family is mentioned in the writings of Marx, Durkheim and Weber, but these writers use it merely as an example. Troeltsch and Wach discuss the religious functions of the family in rather more detail, but too generally and sometimes from a too limited viewpoint. They are interested in the family's functional contribution as a bearer of religious values and behaviour patterns for society. Both stress the contribution made by the dominant theological attitudes of their period to the integrative religious function of the family. Malinowski's treatment of these topics is strictly analytic, but he is mainly interested in showing the functional contribution of the family to society rather than specifically to ecclesiastical organizations.

Investigation of the interdependence of the family and the religious organization (the Church) has brought into prominence the results of certain empirical studies of the last thirty years. These produced an abundance of material to show that families perform particular religious functions only in a particular social framework. Many detailed studies have shown that a change has taken place in most Western industrial societies enabling families to perform religious functions voluntarily. This change is known as secularization. It was secularization which turned the family's contribution to the religious organization into a problem. I shall try to offer some theoretical considerations on the analytic treatment of this situation.

In order to describe and explain the interdependence of religious organizations (Churches) and the family, it is necessary to look generally at the complex relations existing between the phenomena denoted by the two terms "religion" and "family". This can be done theoretically on two levels, on that of *interpersonal relations* and that of *culture*.[1]

Every religion can be regarded on the interpersonal level as a system of differentiated positions whose occupants interact within a framework of institutionally determined expectations. We assume, though cannot show in detail here, that religion as a social system possesses the characteristics of an organization, and that we meet this organization in the various societies in the form of Churches divided into denominations. Churches as religious organizations normally take the form of composite wholes with a clearly defined membership. They show a differentiated internal role structure. Religious organizations offer their members social positions in the organization which are variously valued according to the goals of the organization (which produces the organization's vertical structure). Access to these positions is also carefully regulated (baptism, confirmation, theological study,

[1] On this, see L. Vaskovics, "Religion und Familie—soziologische Problemstellung und Hypothesen", in J. Wössner (ed.), *Religion im Umbruch* (Stuttgart, 1972).

etc.). In these respects there is very little difference between religious and any other organizations. Religious organizations
differ from other (e.g., political) organizations mainly in their
organizational goals. The goals of religious organizations are
rooted in the value and norm systems of the various religions and
have to do with the maintenance and propagation of these
systems. The goal of these organizations is to influence the
behaviour and attitudes of members of the society in the direction of their institutionalized value and norm systems.[2]

From the point of view of interpersonal relations, we may
regard the family as a simple social system with the characteristics of a unique sort of group. On the analytical level of interpersonal relations we are therefore dealing with the interdependence of complex religious organizations (Churches) and groups
of a special sort (families). On the analytical level of culture we
are dealing with two institutions, the institution of religion and
that of the family. Both institutions offer particular possibilities
for satisfying basic human needs in particular ways. In their
effect on the members of a society, both institutions appear as
complexes of connected expectations. These expectations have to
do with a particular category of individual behaviour and attitudes.

Although the expectations of the two institutions relate to the
same category of behaviour and attitudes, this behaviour and
these attitudes (as ways of satisfying needs) give rise to different
goals and means. This produces competition between the two
institutions as a result of the conflicts produced by the different
expectations in the people aiming at the goals. If it is possible to
harmonize the structures of expectations of the two institutions,
not only can this competition be avoided but the ease with which
the expectations can be imposed and the effectiveness of the
sanctions, for both institutions, can also be considerably increased.

I believe that this concept of competition provides the best
way of understanding and explaining the historical interdependence of religious organizations (meaning Churches differentiated
by denomination) and family social systems. I also maintain that

[2] On this, see the explanations of the term "normative organizations",
in A. Etzioni (ed.), Complex Organizations—A Sociological Reader (New
York, 1961), pp. 10 ff.

*religious organizations have always tried to influence the institu-
tions of marriage and the family and to bring the family, as a
group of a special sort, under their social control.*

From their very beginnings, the Christian Churches have made
efforts to derive norms for the goals of marriage and the family
from their value systems and to impose them. The result of these
efforts was the appearance of a special type of family institution,
the institution of Christian marriage and the Christian family.
This institution of Christian marriage and the Christian family
may be described as a system of interrelated role expectations deriving from the value systems of the Christian Churches. In this
institution, not only the meaning and nature of marriage (as a
sacrament or divine law), but also the end of marriage (the pro-
creation and education of children) are reinterpreted in contrast
to the profane institution of marriage and the family.

From this particular valuation of the nature and end of marriage there follow the specific role expectations of the institution
of Christian marriage and the Christian family. These include
role expectations determined by the ritual of the marriage ceremony, the requirements of the indissolubility of the marriage,
fidelity between the partners, the obligation to have children and
the obligation on the parents to bring up their children within
the norm and value system of the Church, and the expectation
that marriage should be monogamous.

These role expectations of the Christian institution of marriage
and the family were reinforced by the religious organization
with heavy sanctions. Formally these were organized religious
sanctions, such as refusal of particular religious services, exclusion
from the religious organization, etc., but they also had the character of social sanctions and often had serious consequences for
those who suffered them even in non-religious areas of activity.

In the course of centuries, the forms of these sanctions have of
course changed, but in the intention of the Christian Churches
their purpose has remained the same, to integrate religious values
and norms into the institution of marriage and the family and
to influence the behaviour and attitudes of members of families
by means of these values and norms.

Let us now consider the question why religious organizations
have been (and are) concerned to make the institution of mar-

riage and the family conform to their values and norms and to bring the family as a social group under their control.

The answer to this question can be summed up in the following sentence. *Religious organizations are anxious to influence the institution of marriage and the family and to bring the members of families under their social control because the recruitment and social and religious placing of the members of religious organizations depend on the performance of certain functions by the family.*

The primary and most general aim of a religious organization is to establish religion in society as an institution. The question this raises for a Church is how the members of a society can be induced to satisfy their religious needs in the ways provided by this religious institution.

In a so-called pluralistic society, in which religious values and norms compete with other values and norms of the culture, religious organizations face another (and presumably prior) question: how can religious needs be stimulated in members of a society? Or, how can the new generation be made to interiorize existing values of the culture and regard them as worth striving for? Only when individuals regard or feel values as worth their striving for does the second question become relevant: how are these individuals to attain these phenomena which they now feel to be worth striving for? What particular things must they do if they want to pursue values? Religious organizations (like all other organizations) also have to answer a third question, how their members can be induced to keep and perform their roles.

To sum up, like other organizations, religious organizations (Churches) have a threefold task: to win members, to induce them to stay and to ensure that they play their roles.[3] As we mentioned previously, the attempts of the religious organizations to carry out this task successfully creates tensions between the institution of religion and the institution of the family on the one hand and religious organizations and families on the other. The reason for this is that in every society families perform functions which can considerably restrict the religious organizations in the

[3] Cf. R. Mayntz, *Soziologie der Organisationen* (Rheinbach bei Hamburg, 4th edn., 1969).

successful accomplishment of their tasks; these functions are re-production, socialization and placing.

Every society attempts to ensure, by means of legitimacy rules, that children are born into complete families and are socialized by their parents. Since the personality system and the social system of the family can be shown to be intimately related, the family has a key position in the transmission of the society's basic value system. The nuclear family is, as a result of various structural features, particularly well placed in the social system as a whole to perform the first and most important stage of social-ization.[4] On the other hand, legitimacy rules and the processes of socialization within the family have particular effects on the pro-cess of the social placing of the child. By "placing" here is meant the process by which a person is given particular positions in a society (in work, in a Church, in associations, etc.).[5]

In view of these functions, religious organizations have always tried to integrate this unique group, the family, into the ecclesi-astical organization and channel its functions in the direction of the organization's goals.

It can easily be shown that Christian organizations have tried to solve their recruitment problems by drawing directly on the reproductive function of the family. Denominational endogamy rules (the expectation that members of a denomination will marry within the denomination) are meant to solve the problem of re-cruiting new members. Interdenominational marriages endanger the ecclesiastical placing of the child. The same motive explains the fact that members of the Churches are socialized into accep-tance of the institutionally prescribed end of marriage (pro-creation) and required to promise at the marriage ceremony to comply with it. Church members are also required to bring up the children they produce in the value and norm system of the Church. This is presupposed by baptism, which normally takes place immediately after birth. The bringing forward of baptism to infancy has made natural reproduction almost automatically the addition of a new member to the Church. Statistics show that the connection of this ecclesiastical placing function of the family

[4] Cf. T. Parsons and R. F. Bales, *Family, Socialization and Interaction Process* (New York, 1950), pp. 35 ff.

[5] F. Neidhardt, *Die Familie in Deutschland* (1966), p. 65.

with its reproductive function is still remarkably effective. The proportion of the members of the Christian Churches who are baptized later, in adolescence or adulthood, is minimal. In other words, the problem of the recruitment of members for the Christian Churches has been solved by combining the reproductive function of the family with the institution of baptism. Most Church legitimacy rules also have the function, in combination with denominational endogamy rules, of ensuring the continuity of the religious organization through the ecclesiastical placing of the child.

Once recruitment of the new member is ensured by birth and baptism, there is a second problem to be solved. This is making the values offered by religious institutions to their members standards of individual action. Members do not have to be socialized in the value and norm system of the Church until they have become members.

Religious organizations have known for a very long time what psychology, psychoanalysis and sociology have only discovered in the last forty years, that the family plays a pre-eminent part in the translation of cultural values into personal ideals, in their translation into the individual's personality structure. This is the only explanation for the way in which the Christian Churches ever since their foundation have tried to make use of the socialization functions of the family for their own internal socialization goals. The Christian Churches (though not only they) maintain institutional role expectations the purpose of which is to make the family take over the religious socialization of the children.

Many empirical studies have clearly shown the functions performed by families on behalf of religious organizations.[6] It can be shown, first, that even in our industrial society the family performs important placing functions for individual religious organizations. The Churches still depend for their membership mainly on the placing function of families. The denominational adherence of parents largely determines the denominational adherence of their children.

[6] I have collected the most important results of these studies in my book *Familie und religiöse Sozialisation* (Vienna, 1970).

Families also perform very important placing functions within the various Churches. Religious organizations offer their members various positions. Whether or not the members possess the appropriate role expectations and so can occupy these positions depends largely on whether they were confronted in childhood and youth with religious role expectations (and if so which), and which religious values and what role behaviour they internalized in the family.

There are many empirical indications that in Western industrial societies the transmission of religious values and norms is more and more becoming a voluntary function, since the religious organizations are no longer able to keep families under their social control. Where the family previously acted as a functional unit for the Churches, performing reproduction, socialization and placing, social changes in industrial societies have introduced a differentiation into the functions performed on behalf of the Churches by families. A certain number of the families of Church members continues to perform all three functions (reproduction, socialization and religious placing) on behalf of the Church, even in the changed social conditions. A second type of family performs the reproductive function, but no longer socializes Church role behaviour, which creates problems for the Churches in their attempts to attain their goals. A third category of family has been recognized more recently, namely one established by Church members but unwilling to perform ecclesiastical reproduction: i.e., the children are not baptized.

As a result of this relative independence of families from religious organizations, ecclesiastical norms and values are being transmitted by families selectively, i.e., on criteria of acknowledged need, subject to the approval and choice of those who determine the content of socialization (the parents). This means that in virtue of their part in socialization families are in a position to influence the value and norm systems of religious organizations and so to influence religion itself *as an institution*.

To sum up, we have seen that by performing particular functions the family, as a group of a particular sort, is in a position to have an important and lasting influence on: (1) the *membership* of religious organizations; (2) the *distribution of the members* among various categories of religious and social position within a religious organization; and (3) the structure of religious institutions. This has also shown us the reason for the constant efforts of religious organizations, such as both Catholic and Protestant Churches, to influence the institution of marriage and the family and to bring families under their social control.

Translated by Francis McDonagh

Gregor Siefer

Ecclesiological Implications of Weber's Definition of "Community"

IT SEEMS to be characteristic of our present-day situation that the approximation of community (*Gemeinschaft*) in the larger sense and community in the ecclesial sense (*Gemeinde*), as laid claim to or devoutly wished for in the traditional self-understanding of the Church, is continually decreasing. Yet, often in complete contrast to the draining of emotional content from the notion of "parish community", new forms of community develop with quite distinct though often very secular nucleii, drawing their initial impulse mostly from acute conflict or necessity, and— given favourable conditions (one of which is usually an imaginative and energetic organizer)—achieving permanence and consistency.[1]

I

In view of this development, it seems appropriate to look again at the work of Max Weber, who was pre-eminently able to elicit from a mass of detailed historical material the processes by which co-operative and dominative systems came into being. The function of "religious" objectives and their mediative mechanisms clearly played a central part in those processes; in this connection the use of, and distinction between, the terms *Gemeinde* and *Gemeinschaft* in Weber's works are also relevant to the present situation.

[1] See especially Andrew Greeley, "The Persistence of Community", *Concilium*, Jan. 1973 (American edn., Vol. 81).

I must stress from the start the fact that Weber very rarely uses the word "community" (*Gemeinschaft*) in an abstract sense, and prefers concrete and dynamic qualifications; hence he speaks primarily of "political communities", of "community (or communal) behaviour", and above all of "communization" (*Vergemeinschaftung*).[2]

Since neither *Gemeinde* nor *Gemeinschaft* is defined as a fundamental term, yet both are used in central contexts in Weber's works, I cannot avoid relatively frequent citation of his works.

In examining the relation of the two terms, one notices a remarkable ambivalence. *Gemeinschaft* is conceivable without *Gemeinde*, but on no account *Gemeinde* without *Gemeinschaft*. If this second case does arise, it is only as a calcified relic of a former *Gemeinschaft*, as a reduction to a mere unit of administration. That does not exclude the possibility (as in older German usage) of the occasional use of the two words as synonymous.[3]

Even Max Weber offers (at least in his chapter on "Charismatic Rule") a similar definition when he speaks of the community formed under the rule of domination as an "emotional communization".[4]

The problematical aspect of this all but identical conception of the two terms is apparent essentially only in regard to the establishment phase of a charismatic union. The "normalization of charisma"—that is, the attempt to preserve the small community (*Gemeinde*) as such indefinitely—already has to change its nature: especially through the necessary resolution of the question of who is to succeed the bearer of the charism once he is gone. There are various answers (revelation, designation, and so on); but the most relevant to the present context is the objectification

[2] A certain distancing from the mythologization initiated by Tönnies of the notion *Gemeinschaft*="community" (as opposed to *Gesellschaft*="society") seems undeniable; especially since, in the preliminary notes to the *Soziologische Grundbegriffe*, in addition to sensible remarks on Jaspers, Simmel, Stammler and Gottl, there is a reference to "the fine work of F. Tönnies".

[3] Cf. T. Geiger, "Gemeinschaft" in A. Vierkandt (ed.), *Handwörterbuch der Soziologie* (Stuttgart, 1959 [1931]), p. 173.

[4] *Wirtschaft und Gesellschaft* (Studienausgabe), I, II (Berlin and Cologne), 1964 [1921] (henceforth cited as *WuG*), *WuG* I, p. 180.

of charisma as a "charism of office": "The faith in legitimacy attaches no longer to the person, but to the acquired qualities and to the efficacy of the hierurgical acts. The most important examples are the priestly charism bestowed or confirmed by anointing, consecration or the laying on of hands, and the royal charism by anointing and crowning. The indelible character means a detachment of the charismatic faculties of office from the personal qualities of the priest."[5]

Here a paradox is already discernible: that community (*Gemeinde*) on the one hand, as a permanent structured relationship of a number of people, clearly develops from a communal relation to these people to one another (religious attachment, comradeship in war, living as neighbours, and so on); that on the other hand, however, every attempt to ensure that this is a permanent relationship affects that very communal character of the relationship which is to be preserved: "The neighbourhood (*Gemeinschaft*) is the aboriginal basis of the *Gemeinde*—a structure supported in the full sense . . . only in relation to a political collectivity comprehending a number of neighbourhoods."[6]

At least three new components of definition are indicated here: quantitative growth; and, accordingly, the economization and rationalization of the collective action; and, finally, the fact that the action itself evokes a political action. For: ". . . [the *Gemeinde*] itself can also, when it controls a 'territory' such as the 'village', represent the basis for a political collectivity; and, above all, in the sense of progressive communization, can include in the collectivity all kinds of activities (from school education and religious duties to the systematic housing of essential craftsmen) or receive them as an assigned duty from the political community."[7]

Almost imperceptibly, the term *Gemeinde* has received its communal-political emphasis: the community as a small political administration unit with specific self-government tasks demarcated and distinguished from the ecclesio-sociological concept of the parish. That both meanings were [in German] for a long time actually and notionally identical explains why the word *Gemeinde* can attain to its due precision only when used in a specific context.

[5] *WuG* I, p. 184.   [6] *WuG* I, p. 282.   [7] *WuG* I, p. 282.

II

If we retain the notion of "neighbourliness", then even in the ethical aspect a fundamental identity of the religious and the political community (*Gemeinde*) becomes apparent. Yet this (if at all) ultimately applies only to the initial phase of establishment. Every distribution of possibilities and positions of power connected with a permanent institutional arrangement endangers neighbourliness. Weber himself speaks of the "failure in principle of the postulate of neighbourliness when faced with the harsh reality of the economic world".[8] A little later he says: "But the more the priesthood tries to organize itself independently over against the political power and the more rational its ethics becomes, the more this original position shifts. The contradiction between the preaching of loving behaviour between brethren and the glorification of war in regard to outsiders was of course of no decisive effect in disestablishing the martial virtues, for it was possible to distinguish between a 'just' and an 'unjust' war—a pharisaical product foreign to the old, authentic war ethic. Far more important was the rise of community religions of politically disarmed nations domesticated by priests, such as the Jews, and the establishment of broad strata (which were at least relatively unwarlike but increasingly significant—where they organized themselves autonomously) for the support and ascendancy of the priesthood. The priesthood had to enjoin the specific virtues of these strata much more exclusively than they did. Simplicity, patient resignation to necessity, humble acceptance of the established authority, and amiable forgiveness and understanding towards injustice, were in fact the very virtues which assisted subjection to the dispensation of the ethical God and the priests themselves."[9]

This compressed account of two thousand years of Church history makes three factors clear. Firstly, we have to find out under what conditions the *Gemeinschaft* becomes a *Gemeinde*, and in what respect these notions begin to be distinct from one another in a differentiated—that is, a more rational—society. Secondly, there is evidence for the rise and extension of a religious leadership caste, a priesthood, attempting to establish itself not only

[8] *WuG* I, p. 456.   [9] *WuG* I, p. 457.

over against the "laity", but as distinct from the political leadership. Thirdly, we have to understand the "rational" bridging of
the gap between claim and reality in the ethical realm (cf. also
the development of the prohibition against usury).

Some explanations are also offered of the differentiation between, and consolidation of, secular and spiritual power—
whether in the form of the Church State or the State Church (not
to speak of that perhaps most rational form of co-operation—the
concordat).

III

However conclusive all these explanations seem at first sight,
we still have to inquire into the conditions which could give
rise to this process. Weber has a specific explanation:

"In fact the religiousness of the early Christians was an urban
religiosity; the significance of Christianity increased under otherwise equal conditions, as Harnack has shown quite convincingly,
with the size of the town. In the Middle Ages, fidelity to the
Church, like sectarian religiousness, quite specifically developed
on the basis of the cities. It is quite improbable that an organized
communal religiousness like that of the early Christians could
have developed as it did develop, outside an urban (i.e., urban in
the Western sense) community life. It presupposes that violation
of the taboo barriers between clans, that concept of office, that
notion of the *Gemeinde* as an 'institution', of a corporate structure serving an objective purpose which strengthened that religiousness and made its reception very much easier by the city
development of the European Middle Ages. It also presupposes
existing conceptions. But such given conceptions evolved fully
only on the basis of Mediterranean culture—especially Hellenistic
and (eventually) Roman city law. But the qualities specific to
Christianity as an ethical religion of redemption and personal
piety had their real forcing-ground in the city, where they continually evoked new impulses."[10]

This seems to contradict the current experience according to
which the rise of the great cities of the modern age meant the
decline of traditional religions. Even if we leave open the ques-

[10] *WuG* I, p. 371.

tion of whether this thesis (taken mainly from French sociography) is at all appropriate, we still have to ask whether "the
city" itself was the cause of such a development, or only the
place in which such changes in consciousness and behaviour were
first visible, socially incident, and measurable (above all in terms
of that unduly prized indicator, church attendance figures).

Much more important is the historical question of whether
specific forms of religious organizational structure (which for
various reasons are today again in decline) were not first able to
develop in the city. That is precisely what Weber states: "For . . .
their inhabitants, the ancient cities were primarily voluntary col-
lectivizations and confederations of bodies of individuals partly
of a primarily tribal and partly a primarily . . . military character,
which were schematized into the later urban divisions according
to administrative and technical aspects. The cities of the ancient
world were sacrally exclusive not only for those without but for
those within, as against those who belonged to none of the
federated clans (the plebeians); for that very reason they remained
divided into initially highly exclusive cultic unions. In this aspect
of noble tribal confederations the ancient cities were fairly close
to the southern European cities of the early Middle Ages. . . .
Within their walls every noble clan had its own redoubt, or one
shared with others. Yet in the medieval cities (and this was very
important) there was no remnant—as still discernible in antiquity
—of a *sacred* exclusivity of clans in relation to one another and
the outside world: a consequence of that historically noteworthy
process in Antioch (justifiably stressed by Paul in Galatians) by
which Peter practised (ritual) communion with uncircumcised
brethren. In the ancient cities this ritual exclusivity had already
weakened to the point of complete disappearance. . . . In middle-
and north-European medieval cities this decline was present
from the beginning, and the clans very soon lost all significance
as urban constituencies. The city became a confederation of *individual* burghers (fathers of families), so that the inclusion of
the citizen in extra-urban communities (*Gemeinschaften*) lost
practically all significance in regard to the city community.
Christianity, which became the religion of nations whose
traditions were all profoundly convulsed, and did so precisely because of the weakness or the lack of magic and taboo

barriers among them, finally devalued and broke the religious significance of all such clan bonds. The often quite important role of the ecclesial community (*Gemeinde*) in the technico-administrative structures of the medieval cities, is only one of many symptoms of the heavy implication of those characteristics of the Christian religion which were responsible for dissolving the clan ties, and which were therefore fundamentally significant for the formation of the medieval city."[11]

The principal consequence of the foregoing seems to be: the importance of "Pauline" Christianity for the rise of the communal city (no longer marked by clan adherence) as the location (and almost as the way of life) of a new social figure—the burgher. Associated with that is the moulding of the Western city as a *Gemeinde* (community), as a democratic collectivity with an in principle equal sharing in government by all citizens. The historical roots of the idea of democracy are to be found here. With the successful functioning of the political community there was a gradual resolution of the basic religious situation, just as the Calvinist merchant came gradually to see profit no longer as a sign of his justification, but as the very goal of his activity.[12]

IV

"Calvinism"—that is, the historic division of the Church—indicates a process which most emphatically had to do with the development of community religiousness. The division of Christianity into different, competing, or even mutually inimical Churches in fact reproduced a situation that had been characteristic of the sacrally divided city of the ancient world and its competing clans. The specific gain of Christianity—sacred openness—was once again lost; the social (and therefore also religious) consequences of this process were concealed for centuries by the religional demarcation of influence deriving from the Augsburg Religious Peace of 1555.

"The relations between political power and religious com-

[11] *WuG* I, pp. 945 ff.
[12] *Gesammelte Aufsätze zur Religionssoziologie*, I–III (Tübingen, 1956 [1920] (henceforth abbreviated as *RS*), *RS* I, p. 197.

munity (*Gemeinde*), giving rise to the notion of 'confession' (or 'denomination'), form part of the analysis of 'rule' (or 'domination'). We can confirm that community religiousness is a variously though unambiguously expressed and unstable phenomenon. I would speak of it only in cases where the laity (1) are societized into a *lasting* community (*Gemeinschaft*) activity, whose progress they (2) also influence *actively* in one way or another. A mere administrative district which defines the priests' competencies is a parish but not a community (*Gemeinde*)."[13]

Accordingly, most of the parishes in Western Europe would have largely lost their community-character, and for two reasons. Firstly, they are no longer true communities because, despite all post-conciliar moves such as parish councils, now as before they are organized as parishes in a priests' Church. Secondly, they are not communities because, in contrast to competitive denominations, they largely preserve sacral exclusivity as church organizations (cf. the contention about intercommunion).

The situation is different where most of the competitive "confessions" generally made the prospect of an identification of state and political community (*Gemeinde*) illusory (as in the U.S.A.). That necessarily led to a change in the function of the community membership for the individual, for here it became an almost class-specific qualification, which in the case of religious or social mobility made a change of "Church" too relatively unproblematic, so long as (and that is the decisive factor) the local receiving community agreed.

"When the individual communities (*Gemeinden*) of the same 'confession' come together to form a greater community (*Gemeinschaft*), this is a 'purposive union'; for that reason, the decisive decree must always remain with the individual community (*Gemeinde*): it enjoys the primacy and, inescapably, it enjoys (if the term is permissible) 'sovereignty'. For the same reason, it is always the 'small' community (*Gemeinde*) (the 'ecclesiola' of the Pietists) which seems suitable for these functions. This is the negative aspect of the 'community (*Gemeinde*) principle', which culminates in a rejection of its naturally universalistic and expansive charism of office. The practical significance for the in-

[13] *WuG* I, p. 358.

dividual of this fundamental position of a community (*Gemeinde*) which has come into being by free choice (ballot) is, however, that it legitimizes him in his personal qualification. Everyone then attests that whoever is received satisfies the religio-moral requirements of the community (*Gemeinde*) in accordance with personality-test. It can be of the greatest and even economic consequence for him, if that test is reliable and extends to economically relevant qualities."[14]

It is different where the lack of competitive denominations, that is the preservation of confessional homogeneity (as, for instance, in Poland), hardly obstructs the wear-and-tear of secularization, yet sacral openness, in the case of a conflict with the State, makes the Church a refuge for all those seeking protection, and precisely when the character of the priests' Church is retained, because only then (if the priests are in a strong position) can a protective function of the Church as a "salvific institution" become in any way practicable.

If the goal of making the *Gemeinde* a *Gemeinschaft* is retained, there seem to be only two choices—either a cancellation of denominational competition, that is, ecumenism in the sense of the effacement of confessional delimitations at least among Christian Churches, or a specialization of the major Churches into perhaps loose groupings of local communities, which would be tantamount to approval for the priests' Church, although the lay element would be much more heavily involved. But this would certainly mean a great change in the function of community membership as far as the individual is concerned.

V

Since any cessation of confessional competition through a fusion of churches appears to be as impossible as the prospect of establishing a new community consciousness of parishes, the established Church apparatus is still based primarily on the "people". But that means almost of necessity a preference for all strategies which guarantee a strengthening of priestly (as opposed to lay) positions. In certain situations, reasoned arguments for that viewpoint can be found, but as a rule it is dangerously erroneous, especially since

[14] *WuG* I, pp. 917 ff.

the possibility of a "popular" (though authentically baseless) priests' Church is by no means inconceivable.

"In China, where the state cult also ignored the needs of individuals, magic was never suppressed by a major redemptive prophecy or native saviour-religion.... Taoism was only an organization of sorcerers, and Buddhism in its imported form was no longer the redemptive religiosity of the early-Buddhist period in India, but the magic and mystagogic practice of a monastic organization. In both cases, therefore, at least for the laity, the decisive sociological factor was absent: the formation of a religious community. These semi-popular, quasi-magical, aspects of a redemptive religion were therefore as a rule quite unsocial."[15]

The complex of problems in the West today is essentially different: the question is whether it is possible to capture and monopolize the present process of mass-enlightenment and intellectualization—for the priests think of themselves, in contrast to the people, as "intellectuals", even though they may eschew the word. This process of controlling a monopoly of information and decision in regard to the people is also repeated outside the traditional major Churches where politically established, intellectual world-views have reached a no less rigid controlled regulation of everyday life, controlled by party bureaucracies, and in that very process have taken on a quasi-ecclesial character, at least as long as they are in visible competition with traditional Church systems, whose formal socialization pattern they try at least in part to adopt.

Clearly, with increasing social differentiation (and intellectualization), neither the Churches nor the Parties can fulfil and maintain this asserted general competency in all questions of behavioural standards. They usually react ambivalently (with a continual interchange of laxity and rigorism) to "deviations" from the line that has been laid down as true and valid, and thus prepare the way for an organizational pattern which, with its claim of possessing the "true faith", begins to undercut the major system: i.e., the sect—whether the Pharisees, the mendicant orders, the non-conformist Churches or the revisionist Marxists. Weber says of the Pharisees:

[15] *RS* I, p. 511.

"It was from the Pharisees that Paul acquired the technique of propaganda and the creation of an unassailable community. The strong upswing in the Jewish diaspora from the time of the Maccabees and its complete imperturbability in the face of an alien environment, from which they cut themselves off, was to a very great extent the product of their fraternal movement. . . . For the community now becomes the vehicle of religion, no longer the hereditary charism of priests and levites.

"The fraternities held eucharistic celebrations ('love-feasts') of a similar kind, which were certainly models for the later Christian institutions of the same kind. The blessings at meals were also quite similar. The Pharisees also held the very popular water-procession. . . . Above all they produced the synagogue . . . which replaced the priestly-cult for the diaspora Jew, and higher and lower education in the Law, which was fundamental for the shaping of Judaism. Slowly but profoundly they also altered the meaning of the sabbath and feast-days. Instead of the priestly temple-feast (just as I noticed the same thing as a symptom of emancipation among the Brahmins in India), there was the domestic and synagogal feast, and consequently an unavoidable devaluation of sacrifice and of the priesthood, before even the collapse of the second temple. Above all recourse was now had to the legally-versed teacher and no longer to the priest, if one was in outward or inward need or in doubt about ritual duties."[16]

Even though that means that the experience of an "interrupted competency" in questions of advice about living and existential regulation for priests was not a discovery of the modern age, the possibility of forming a community "from below" is a continually new question, for "mere 'feeling' for the common position and its consequences no longer produces [communization]. Only when they [people distinguished by a common characteristic] *direct* their behaviour *towards* one another on the basis of this feeling, does a social relationship arise between them—not only between each one of them and the environment—and 'community' comes into being only to the extent that it bears witness to a felt togetherness."[17]

When, through the present high mobility of individuals and

[16] *RS* I, 2, 3.   [17] *WuG* I, pp. 30 ff.

information, a multiplicity of structures and behavioural forms affecting the consciousness of a great number of individuals develops as a concretization of responsible freedom, the community should really appear as the "father's house" in which there are "many mansions": that is, as the place in which different, indeed contradictory, opinions are found, and find receptive ears and free expression. The new aspect is less in the multitude of variations (they existed earlier—naturally or as regular privileges) but much more in the fact that these variations can occur today in a *single* community.

Tolerance (in actuality sufferance) by existing communities of "deviant" behaviour should be acknowledged as the hallmark of their own survival. A rigid exclusion of change means no more than a reversion to the bond-religiosity which merely preserves pure traditions and which thinks to ensure its stability primarily in a ritualistic securing of its sacral exclusivity. This also has consequences for the ethical behaviour of such a system, to which, for example, the history of the Jews in the midst of Christianity bears long and questionable witness.

VI

Among the multitude of appropriate perspectives and reflections, I find the following results especially deserving of consideration for an ecclesiological "strategy".

1. The possible re-identification of *Gemeinde* and *Gemeinschaft* on the basis of modern high-church systems would be found formally only with a confessional homogeneity, and therefore in the cessation of difference and competition between rival confessions. Rivalry towards the "State" could hardly support such a process in the long run, even though it might perhaps do so for a short while.

2. Both the actual unlikelihood of a quick removal of confessional competitive factors and still more the long experience of the collapse of priestly universal responsibility by reason of the scientization of everyday life, show that reference to "lay needs" —and not only or exclusively those of lay intellectuals—is unavoidable. That "needs" are not only "consumer needs" must be emphasized today. "Need" also and primarily means giving

people a hearing; it refers to co-operation, co-determination—and thus means being taken seriously in a process of direct, actual contact despite all hierarchical distance.

3. The thesis that the city is the direct cause of the decline of religion and the religious consciousness must be revised. We should not be surprised that the city necessarily stressed the lack of congruence between "agrarian" forms of religiosity and the needs of the city-dweller. The discovery of the special styles proper to a "city" religiousness and the provision of room for their operation is still a task of the "new" community.

At least three consequences now become clear which were already vaguely recognizable. Measured against "false" objectives, they are discriminated against as deviation, way-out situations, and so on.

1. The decentralization of competent decision. Respect for the principle of subsidiarity both in church and local community (not only between the bishop and Rome).

2. Respect for and acceptance of "freely" arising experiments, for the most part subsisting on the outskirts of the traditional communities, or near them (para-communities), which often draw their primary motivation from an experience of the lack of community (*Gemeinschaft*) in the existing parishes (*Gemeinden*).

3. If the above two could still be interpreted as a reduction of "official" activities, then the third consequence would be an equally necessary and difficult task: "conflict processing" instead of (as hitherto) conflict suppression by prohibition. For an unavoidable result of the foregoing development will be conflicts—within communities and between communities; between individuals, generations, decision-makers, and so on. But "conflict processing" means that the forces in the Church which cause offence will remain, and that a change in Church structure will take place above and beyond change in the community: not so that a venerable structure called the Church can survive, but so that the still countless men who have put their trust (and perhaps a faint hope) in it may find in a changing world an answer to the question of the meaning of that same world.

Translated by V. Green